HOLIDAYS
IN
HECK

❖

ALSO BY P. J. O'ROURKE

Modern Manners
The Bachelor Home Companion
Republican Party Reptile
Holidays in Hell
Parliament of Whores
Give War a Chance
All the Trouble in the World
Age and Guile Beat Youth, Innocence, and a Bad Haircut
Eat the Rich
The CEO of the Sofa
Peace Kills
On The Wealth of Nations
Driving Like Crazy
Don't Vote—It Just Encourages the Bastards

P. J. O'ROURKE

HOLIDAYS IN HECK

Atlantic Monthly Press
New York

3/58898

Published simultaneously in Canada
Printed in the United States of America

FIRST EDITION

ISBN-13: 978-0-8021-1985-8

Atlantic Monthly Press
An imprint of Grove/Atlantic, Inc.
841 Broadway
New York, NY 10003

Distributed by Publishers Group West

www.groveatlantic.com

11 12 13 14   10 9 8 7 6 5 4 3 2 1

To Tina,
I owe you a holiday.
And—what the heck—to Lizzie, Lulu, and Cliff

CONTENTS

ACKNOWLEDGMENTS

❖

Sheer amateurism is a reporter's only excuse for traveling without an assignment to do so. Therefore, the pieces in this book were assigned. Many of these assignations came from *Forbes Life*, which is—and I mean this in the best way—the monkey business supplement to *Forbes*, America's preeminent business magazine. *Forbes Life* (originally called *Forbes FYI*) was founded by my excellent friend Christopher Buckley who, in a flash of inspiration, realized that the people who make money reading *Forbes* might occasionally want to blow some. Blowing money is what I do.

My thanks to Christopher and a plug in recompense. He is the first person since Evelyn Waugh to master the agonizingly difficult art of the comic novel. Buy all his books. And my thanks to Patrick Cooke and Richard Nalley who brilliantly followed Christopher's brilliance as editors of *Forbes Life* and to their brilliant boss Bob Forbes, my summer neighbor in New Hampshire's Beige Mountains. Together these gentlemen underwrote my journeys to the Galápagos Islands, the Yangtze, Kyrgyzstan, Hong Kong, Brays Island Plantation, and even my rare opportunity, described in Chapter 19, to stay home.

My wife, Tina, and I were invited to go on the Galápagos excursion by our extraordinary Texas friends Lee and Ramona Bass. But, between invitation and embarkation, Tina turned up pregnant with Buster (whose first appearance in print is recorded in Chapter 3). Doctors forbade Tina from messing around in boats. So I took along my Godson Nick McDonell.

Nick, a New York City boy, was then a freshman at Harvard. This was his first exposure to Republicans en mass, particularly Texas Republicans, and, more particularly, the beautiful teenage daughters of Texas Republicans, who accompanied us on the cruise. Nick is a handsome and engaging young man, and the girls were fascinated by his exotic liberalism. One evening, on my way to the bar, I saw the entire contingent of adolescent Texan females gathered around a table with my Godson. I overheard a mellifluous voice with sugared southern accent say, "Why, *Nick*, you-all just don't *understand* gun control!"

My travels through mainland China and my sojourn with my family in Hong Kong would not have been possible without our peerless friends Dave and Celia Garcia. I've been imposing on their hospitality in the Orient for twenty years. We've shared trips with them to Italy, Spain, and Thailand. And Dave has been a boon companion—coming along for the fun of it—on my reporting trips to Israel, the West Bank, and

Egypt. Once, while we were walking back to the American Colony Hotel in East Jerusalem late at night, a couple of kids tried to heave a Molotov cocktail at us. It fell pathetically short. Dave shouted, "You throw like girls. If you Palestinians want a country, you'd better learn to play baseball."

Speaking of learning things, I owe my—very tenuous— ability to stay on a horse to the worthy Adrian Dangar. If it weren't for him I wouldn't have survived the horseback ride across the mountains of Kyrgyzstan. Although, come to think of it, if it weren't for him I wouldn't have *been* on the horseback ride across the mountains of Kyrgyzstan. So thanks, Adrian, I guess. Anyway, Adrian's Wild and Exotic Ltd. tour company—www.wildandexotic.co.uk—is a splendid operation. He'll talk you into doing all sorts of things that are wild and exotic. But it's all perfectly safe. The last time Adrian led a horse trek across the Serengeti only one of the riders was attacked by a lion and hardly any of his horse was eaten. Adrian also took the author photo for this book, capturing with speed and skill a rare instant when I wasn't falling out of the saddle.

Still speaking of learning things, my wife owes her knowledge of how to shoot me on the fly to our estimable friends at Brays Island Plantation in South Carolina, Perry and Sally Harvey, and to the admirable Hugh and Gay Eaton who first introduced us to Brays. It's the perfect place to retire, which I'll never get to do because my wife knows how to shoot me on the fly.

Another generous source of holidays has been *The Weekly Standard*. I've been a proud contributor since its inception in 1995—though how proud its masters of political deep-thinking—founders Bill Kristol and Fred Barnes, deputy editor Richard Starr, and literary editor Phil Terzian—are of that

I can't say. *TWS* is not the first venue that comes to mind for leisure and travel writing. But now and then conservative virtue needs to take time off. Meanwhile the evils of leftism are notoriously far-flung.

I took some time off in Guadeloupe, with the excuse that the island was voting on the E.U. constitution just then. Being a Neo-Con, I needed no excuse to visit the aircraft carrier USS *Theodore Roosevelt,* go to Kabul, or mock the docents-fluent-in-Newspeak Field Museum in Chicago. I can't remember what excuse I used to get myself to Venice with a room at the Gritti Palace on the magazine's nickel. But it must have been a doozy.

For my visit to the "Big Stick" I thank my distinguished old friend Frank Saul who introduced me to my distinguished new friend Jim Haynes at the Friendly Sons of St. Patrick dinner in Washington, where many bold plans are hatched. This one still seemed like a good idea in the morning. Jim, former general counsel of the Department of Defense during the George W. Bush administration (and how we miss it), arranged the carrier embark. Thank you, Jim, and may the wind be always at your back and may the road rise to meet you. (Whatever the Irish mean by that—sounds like an Irish description of tripping on your shoelaces).

Among the first and best friends I made in Washington was Jim Denton, who gave me the occasion to travel to Afghanistan. Jim runs Heldref Publications and edits *World Affairs*, America's oldest foreign policy publication. He introduced me to Jeff Gedmin, who was then the head of Radio Free Europe/Radio Liberty. Jeff, with the help of executive editor John O'Sullivan, had great success in transcending the genre of government broadcasting. He turned RFE/RL into a network of radio stations to which people listen avidly rather than dutifully. I went to Prague to do a story on RFE/RL for *World Affairs.* As part of that story I visited RFE/RL's Afghan station, Radio Azadi. My journey to Kabul turned out to be a pleasure trip. This, obviously, was due to the people rather than the place. Foremost among these people is M. Amin Mudaqiq, RFE/RL Afghan Bureau Chief. He provided the broadest access, the most wide-ranging introductions, and the warmest hospitality. This gave me material to write a second piece, about Afghanistan itself, for *The Weekly Standard.*

Jim Denton also published, in *World Affairs,* the account of my conversations with manufacturers and entrepreneurs in China. These would have been the mute talking to the deaf if it hadn't been for the help of Celia Garcia, fluent in English, Cantonese, and Mandarin. Additional thanks to Harvey West and Xiaobo Yao-West for even more and even better conversations at their home in Guangzhou.

Search is another magazine from Heldref Publications (a company founded by Jeanne Kirkpatrick and her husband). It's devoted to the science/religion relationship. (They need to talk.) *Search,* under the skilled editorship of Peter Manseau, published the first part of my essay on getting cancer. Having failed to die, there was a second part. This was published in the Dartmouth-Hitchcock Medical Center's newsletter, *Skylight,* an attractive glossy broadsheet that's more interesting than most of what you read in hospital waiting rooms. Not that they keep you waiting long at competent and considerate Dartmouth-Hitchcock. I failed to die as the result of the efforts of virtuoso oncologist Dr. Marc Pipas and maestro radiologist Dr. Bassem Zaki. I thank you both and so do my wife, my children, two out of three of my dogs, and my life insurance company. My health insurance company says they'll get back to you on that. I also owe undying, as it were, gratitude to my incomparable buddy Greg Grip. Greg lives on a lake near the hospital. When he heard that I needed to undergo treatments every weekday, ninety miles from my home, he said, "I'm not telling you that you can stay with me. I'm telling you that I will be deeply offended if you don't." Whereupon he vacated his own bedroom and installed me there, with Elvis-sized bed, giant flat screen TV, and his bird dog to keep me company. You won't get that kind of treatment from from Obama's healthcare plan.

Although I have traveled a lot, I have rarely traveled to the realms of literary respectability. When I did, however, in the pages of *The Atlantic,* I had the rare good fortune to work with editors worthy of respect no matter how respectable they were. First there was the late, much-missed Michael Kelly, then Cullen Murphy, and, after the magazine had moved to Washington, James Bennet, James Gibney, and Don Peck. Under their aegis *The Atlantic* sent me to cover a stupefaction—the Airbus A380—a stupefying—Britain's hunting ban—and the stupid—Disney's House of the Future.

Adrian Dangar took me to the stag hunt on Exmoor and called upon his friends Tom and Margaret Yandle and Astrid St. Aubyn to feed me to surfeit and shelter me in comfort.

The same duties fell to my sterling friend Peter Flynn with whom I toured the giant Airbus A380 and the small, by comparison, city of Toulouse.

When I told the editor of *Ski* magazine, the clever and sagacious Kendall Hamilton, that I wanted to go skiing in Ohio, he didn't laugh. Which was a problem because he was supposed to. But he thought I was kidding. When he realized I was serious, *then* he laughed. And sent me there. This may have been carrying the joke too far.

All of the articles collected here have been rewritten, some of them extensively—in order that this be a book rather than a recycling bin of old magazine pieces. Although, of course, recycling is a good thing. We don't want to pollute the mental environment by leaving discarded piles of old ideas lying around or deplete the mind's natural resources of new thought. However, one story—my failed attempt to get the family to tour Washington, D.C.—has not been published before. This is because, as you may notice, nothing happens in it. At my age and with a bunch of kids, to have nothing happen is a dream come true. Tina and I were able to live the dream because of the wonderful leisure skills of our splendid Washington friends Andy and Denise Ferguson and their children Gillum and Emily; Nick and Mary Eberstadt and their children Rick, Kate, Isabel, and my Goddaughter Alexandra; and Frank and Dawn Saul and their children Natalie, Charlotte, and young Frank. Tina and I thank them.

Tina can thank herself for being married to the peripatetic, or peri*pathetic* as it more properly should be spelled. But it is I who must thank her for putting up with it. And also for *inputting* up with it. She got this book computerized while her husband stood around making exasperated noises and pretending his ignorance and sloth represented a principled stand against the indignities of the digital age.

Many other thanksgivings are to be celebrated. Noble soldier pal Lt. Colonel Mike Schellhammer and I, with the help of beer, have been working on the Introduction's rant against modern air travel for years now.

Liane Emond deciphered my raw manuscripts and entered them into the mysteries of Microsoft Word.

Don Epstein, who has been both my friend and partner in business for three decades, and all the hard-working, good-looking smart people at the Greater Talent Network lecture agency kept finding real work for me in an era when "print journalist" is a synonym for "unemployed." I was a writer for forty years. Now I'm a content provider. And the Internet says, "Content is free." Not at GTN it isn't.

Nor at the Grove/Atlantic publishing house under the intrepid leadership of Morgan Entrekin—my publisher since 1983 and the Best Man at one of my weddings (unfortunately the wrong one). Anyway, we dinosaurs of the printed page are going to fight this comet collision with new media. Notable among the brave combatants: managing editor Michael Hornburg—who manages somehow to manage it all; associate editor Andrew Robinton—with whom all good things are associated; production director Sue Cole—who directs production like Sam Peckinpah directed *The Wild Bunch*; art director Charles Rue Woods—let's dump all those tired old Picassos and hang the book covers of Charles Woods in MOMA; illustrator Daniel Horowitz—the Piero della Francesca of families packed into a car (and thanks as well to camera wizard and good friend James Kegley from whose kind and flattering photo of me Daniel worked); copy editor Susan Gamer—if James Joyce had known about her you'd be able to read *Finnegans Wake*; proofreader Liv Osthus—proof that sainthood awaits those who suffer PJ's spelling; publicity director Deb Seager—Grove/Atlantic's one true celebrity; and Scott Manning of Scott Manning and Associates—Lady Gaga would be *really* famous if she had Scott doing her P.R.

Be of stout heart all of you. Books will survive. I'll tell you why:

- As the Good Kindle says . . .
- There is no frigate like a Kindle.
- Throw the Kindle at him!
- I wonder, wonder, wonder, wonder who? Who scanned in the Kindle of love?
- My life is a charged Kindle.
- "Kindle him, Dano."
- I could Twitter a Kindle about it.

HOLIDAYS
IN
HECK

❖

I have discovered that all human evil comes from this, man's being unable to sit still in a room.

—Pascal

INTRODUCTION

A Former War Correspondent

Experiences Frightening Vacation Fun

❖

After the Iraq War I gave up on being what's known in the trade as a "shithole specialist." I was too old to be scared stiff and too stiff to sleep on the ground. I'd been writing about overseas troubles of one kind or another for twenty-one years, in forty-some countries, none of them the nice ones. I had a happy marriage and cute kids. There wasn't much happy or cute about Iraq.

Michael Kelly, my boss at *The Atlantic,* and I had gone to cover the war, he as an "imbed" with the Third Infantry Division, I as a "unilateral." We thought, once ground operations began, I'd have the same freedom to pester the locals that he and I had had during the Gulf War a dozen years before. The last time I saw Mike he said, "I'm going to be stuck with the 111th Latrine Cleaning Battalion while you're driving your rental car through liberated Iraq, drinking Rumsfeld Beer and judging wet *abeyya* contests." Instead I wound up trapped in Kuwait, bored and useless, and Mike went with the front line to Baghdad, where he was killed during the assault on the airport. Mike had a happy marriage, too, and cute kids the same ages as mine. I called my wife, Tina, and told her that Mike was dead and I was going to Baghdad to take his place. Tina cried about Mike and his widow and his children. But Tina is the daughter of an FBI agent. Until she was fourteen she thought all men carried guns to work. She said, "All right, if you think it's important to go."

It wasn't important. And that was that for war correspondence. I decided to write about pleasant places. Fortunately, my previous assignments—Lebanon, the West Bank, the Soviet Union, apartheid-era South Africa, the jungles of the Philippines, Saudi Arabia, Somalia, Pakistan's Northwest Frontier, Bosnia, Kosovo, etc.—set a low bar for pleasant. Unfortunately I had no experience with pleasure travel. I'd always been where people were shooting each other or wanting to shoot each other or—in the case of my side job as a car journalist—trying to die in horrible wrecks. How, I wondered, does one undertake enjoyably going somewhere enjoyable?

Apparently there are rules about traveling for fun. The first rule is to find the most crowded airplane on an airline that regards its customers as self-loading freight. Bonus points if the cabin crew is jocular about this. Nothing but lukewarm diet soda is to be served and that only on flights longer than three hours in duration. Passengers must be very fat, hold babies on their laps, and make certain the infants are suffering from painful ear infections. Passengers should also bring everything they own onto the plane in wheelie bags and ram these into my knee as they go down the aisle. This luggage is to be dropped on my head after it fails to fit into the overhead bins, then crammed into the under-seat space in front of *my* feet. Everyone, please be sure to insist on having a conversation if I'm trying to read and also sneeze and cough frequently, get up to go to the toilet every five minutes if you're in the window seat in my row, or kick the seat back rhythmically for hours if you're in the row behind. And no matter what your age or the climate at your destination you must dress as if you're a nine-year-old headed for summer camp.Apparently shorts and T-shirts are what one wears when one is having fun. I don't seem to own any fun outfits. I travel in a coat and tie. This is useful in negotiating customs and visa formalities, police barricades, army checkpoints, and rebel roadblocks. "Halt!" say border patrols, policemen, soldiers, and guerrilla fighters in a variety of angry-sounding languages.

I say, "Observe that I am importantly wearing a jacket and tie."

"We are courteously allowing you to proceed now," they reply.

This doesn't work worth a damn with the TSA.

Then there's the problem of writing about travel fun, or fun of any kind. Nothing has greater potential to annoy a reader than a writer recounting what fun he's had. Personally—and I'm sure I'm not alone in this—I have little tolerance for fun when other people are having it. It's worse than pornography and almost as bad as watching the Food Channel. Yet in this manuscript I see that, as a writer, I'm annoying my reader self from the first chapter until the last sentence. I hope at least I'm being crabby about it. Writers of travelogues are most entertaining when—to the infinite amusement of readers—they have bad things happen to them. I'm afraid the best I can do here is have a bad attitude.

That's not hard for me. What is this thing called fun? To judge by traveling with my wife and daughters it has something to do with shopping for clothes. But I already have clothes; otherwise I'd be standing there in Harrod's naked. Or maybe it has to do with eating in fancy restaurants. I like a good meal and often, in the midst of one, I'll begin to reminisce about dining on raw lamb brains in Peshawar, and suddenly nobody's eating. There is the romantic side of a romantic getaway to be considered. Mrs. O. got quite snuggly on a moonlit night in Venice in the back of one of those beautiful teak *motoscafo* water taxis, speeding from the Piazza San Marco to Lido beach. Speaking for myself, however, I'd just as soon be home in bed without the lagoon sewage spray and the boat driver sneaking peeks. And a kid's idea of fun is a frightening amusement park ride. I'm a professional coward. I make my living by being terrified. I shouldn't pay somebody when I get on Space Mountain; somebody should pay me when I get off.

The word "fun" is not found anywhere in the Bible—no surprise to a Catholic. According to the *Oxford English Diction-ary*, "fun" first occurs circa 1700 as slang for a trick, hoax, or practical joke. It may derive from the Middle English "fon," meaning to cheat. Dr. Johnson called it "a low cant word."

In his *Dictionary of Catch Phrases*, the eminent lexicographer Eric Partridge lists a number of expressions concerning fun. They don't indicate that much is being had. "Ain't we got fun!" comes from the lyrics of a 1920 song by Richard A. Whiting: "Not much money/But, oh, honey/Ain't we got fun!" Probably not for long. "Having fun?" is a question posed only to those who clearly aren't. A more kindly version is the existential query that the cartoonist Bill Griffith had Zippy the Pinhead make, "Are we having fun yet?" which Eric Partridge died too soon to note. "It's all good clean fun" means it isn't. And we mustn't forget "more fun than a barrel of monkeys." How long have the monkeys been in the barrel? Does the barrel have airholes?

Googling "fun" in March 2011, I got, first: "Due to a scheduling conflict, **fun** will not be performing at the June 25th Panic at the Disco show in Portland, OR." And, second: "FunBrain is the #1 site for online educational games for kids of all ages (math, grammar, science, spelling, history)."

And *Bartlett's* has only a dozen quotations concerning fun, none of which are fun to quote except a stanza from the poem "Hi!" by Walter de la Mare, which takes me back to my days as a shithole specialist:

> *Bang! Now the animal*
> *Is dead and dumb and done.*
> *Nevermore to peep again, creep*
>   *again, leap again,*
> *Eat or sleep or drink again, oh,*
>   *what fun!*

I

REPUBLICANS EVOLVING

The Galápagos Islands, April 2003

❖

It is sometimes thought that Republicans are not environmentally conscious, that we are not concerned about the planet or, as we call it, the outdoors. This is not true. We love the outdoors and carefully instruct our children in its manifold splendors. For example, the son of a Republican friend of mine, when asked by his preschool teacher if he could name the four seasons, proudly said, "Dove, ducks, deer, and quail!"

We Republicans respect and revere the natural world— and all its natural laws and truths we hold to be self-evident. We're particularly respectful of that aspect of the natural world known as Darwinian selection, whatever you may have heard to the contrary in our churches. Creationism is all well and good on Sunday, but it's "survival of the most market-oriented" the rest of the week and also in the voting booth. Thus it was that some Republican friends of mine and I made a pilgrimage to that ecological treasure and living monument to Charles Darwin, the Galápagos Islands.

Several million years ago the Galápagos Islands popped, volcanically, out of the Pacific Ocean. The South American mainland being six hundred miles away and nothing else nearby, each island was a tabula rasa. Various birds, lizards, sea mammals, and seeds blew in and washed up. Biological colonization occurred by dumb luck. Very dumb luck, to judge by how the local critters flap, crawl, and paddle up and present themselves to visiting omnivore bipeds for examination of gustatory potential. Pirates, whalers, and other non-members of the World Wildlife Federation had an estimated 100,000 friendly, curious Galápagos giant tortoises for lunch.

Isolation allowed unusual life-forms to flourish. It's an experiment we all made, when we were single, with Chinese take-out left in the refrigerator for six months. Interesting what happens when all the ecological niches except the shelf the beer is on are empty. General Tso's chicken can develop into something that fills the whole fridge. Darwin may have noticed this in the fridge of the HMS *Beagle*. Anyway, when the *Beagle* arrived in the Galápagos, Darwin—perhaps after a heavy lunch of giant tortoise and beer—formulated his theory of evolution, which may be restated for Republicans as: If you're slow and edible and I have a gun, the situation will evolve.

Unfortunately, now that the *Beagle* has been decommissioned, going to the Galápagos in style is something of a problem. For the most part the only way to see the islands is as a tourist on a cruise. There is a kind of tourist who takes this kind of cruise. This tourist loves nature in unnatural ways. An awful prospect presented itself of vegan fare at the captain's table and conversation about earth being in the balance, never mind that the earth has a mass of 5.97×10^{24} kilograms while Al Gore weighs little more than 250 pounds.

Fortunately, I know a Texan couple with the Texan energy and Republican ingenuity needed to tackle this downside of a Galápagos excursion. George and Laura (not their real names) spent a year juggling the busy schedules of fifty-some pals who adore nature's glories especially when a covey of them is pointed by our bird dogs. George and Laura then balanced the juggled schedules with the sailing dates of the MS *Polaris,* owned by that paragon organizer of exotic trips, Lindblad Expeditions. We arrived in the Galápagos not as tourists but as a floating house party. We had booked the whole ship. A vessel that might have flown the Greenpeace unjolly roger now, in effect, hoisted the happy burgee of a yacht. If our dinner seating included members of PETA, we could tell the cruise director, "Throw these vegetarians to the sharks!" Not that Lindblad Expeditions has cruise directors. Lindblad has naturalists with advanced degrees in wildlife biology. Each day these guides took us, by Zodiac boats, to a different Galápagos island. There they delivered talks on Galápagos flora and fauna, giving us important ecology lessons.

On Fernandina Island, our guide said, "The vestigial wings of the flightless cormorant evolved due to a lack of natural predators." Significant glances were exchanged among my shipmates. Being Republicans, we *are* natural predators. A nearby flightless cormorant spread stumpy and functionless appendages that looked to make him eligible for membership in the Feather Club for Birds.

"That's what happens to you without free-market competition," said Laura.

"The flightless cormorant is endemic to the Galápagos islands of Fernandina and Isabela," said our guide. ("Endemic" is wildlife biologist talk for "doesn't get out much" or "stuck there.")

"Notice how close we can get to the birds, even when they are nesting," our guide continued. "This is because they have no experience with humans; they are truly wild."

"Of course!" said a Dallas lawyer. "I should have realized that a long time ago—in my junior year of college—wild equals stupid."

It was an insight that dominated shipboard sundowner gin and tonic chatter.

"Into the stupid blue yonder."

"Call of the stupid."

"Stupid Kingdom."

"Stupid thing, you make my heart sing, you make everything . . . stupid."

The Galápagos are an Ecuadorian national park and a UNESCO World Heritage Site. Strict preservation of the pristine stupidity of the wilderness allowed us to experience a close communion with the animal world that you can't get even from Rover, no matter how stupid he is. The endemic waved albatross let us in on its every Dr. Phil moment. The birds mate for life, then immediately separate. They go off alone for months at sea and return to Española Island in the Galápagos to breed. But before the albatross husband gets back together with his albatross wife, he rapes the other wives. There is an elaborate reconciliation with squawking and slapping of beaks ending in mutual embrace—perfect for daytime bird television. They have an egg, probably to strengthen the relationship. Then they take turns sitting on it for up to a week at a time. When Al Junior is hatched he gets as much as four and a half pounds of food regurgitated down his throat in a single feeding. By five months the chick weighs more than its parents. Feminist issues, family leave, childhood obesity—on Española we had found a place where Hillary Clinton truly could make a difference.

Speaking of objects of ridicule, there is the foolishly waddling, risibly yclept blue-footed booby. The boobies' webbed toes are as funny-colored as a UN flag. Their mating dance is a disco polka. They give each other pebbles.

Boobies share their inshore feeding waters with the noble frigate bird. The frigate birds soar and loop on vast scimitar wings and grace the sky with acrobatics. It's impossible not to admire the one and disparage the other, until it's time for work. The boobies are skilled divers. Plunging from a hundred feet in the air into water sometimes only eighteen inches deep, they harvest whole schools of fish. Then the frigate birds grab the boobies by their tails in midair and bite them and shake them until the boobies cough up their food. "Back on the ground," said our guide, "the male frigate birds have a very large red throat pouch which they puff full of air to attract . . ."

"Voters, I'll bet," said a woman who'd survived a political appointment in the Bush père administration. "Observe the frigate birds," she said, "and you know everything you need to know about Democratic presidential candidates."

"The blue-footed boobies need re-branding," said a marketing consultant from New York. "Those feet—they've a skateboard sneaker franchise crying out for a licensing deal."

"Look," said our guide, "a lava gull." He pointed to a bird that was more like a dove than the airborne sanitation engineer that we call a gull. "They're very rare," said the guide, "maybe only four hundred in the world."

"They must be delicious," said one of our more avid bird-hunters. Our shipboard party was of the opinion that extinction probably has as much to do with flavor as with pollution or climate change. Whenever a new creature was spotted, our first question was, "How do they taste?"

It took all week to get one of our guides to admit that he knew how giant tortoise tastes. Not personally, of course, but he was born in the Galápagos and "a long, long time ago my parents had some."

"Well?" we said.

"Good."

The food on the *Polaris* was good, too, albeit lacking in turtle chops and breast of lava gull. The crew was cheerful. The cabins were not too boat-size. And every night the Lindblad guides delivered further informative talks on Galápagos flora and fauna, giving us more important ecology lessons.

Some of us preferred to spend the evenings on the fantail in consultation with Professor Dewar's and Dr. Monte Cristo. Inside, a Lindblad guide was explaining how young the Galápagos Islands are, in geological time. Outside, George was suggesting that setting our watches to geological time could lessen stress and keep *us* young. "I'll get back to you on that right away—in geological time."

Mornings we snorkeled—an abrupt and effective hangover cure. Commercial fishing is banned in the Galápagos. The island waters are a fish Calcutta. So many giant angelfish appeared that I felt like the bubbling deep-sea diver in the aquarium of a pet store that just can't make a sale.

Tiny, silver pizza-toppers swam in schools the size of Little Italy. Parrot fish, damselfish, and wrasses exhibited the same obliviousness to our presence as the wave albatross and, mercifully, so did the white-tipped sharks (who'd already gorged themselves, perhaps, on vegetarians). Manta rays in watery flight winged by and had a look, as did gringo fish, so called by the locals because they're pale in the water and turn bright red in the sun.

Back in the Zodiac (and rather pink ourselves) we were told by our guide, "You'll notice the puffer fish is particularly friendly—because it is poisonous."

"Typical," said a Houston hostess who has to endure a lot of political fund-raisers.

Young sea lions came out and dived with us. They did barrel rolls around our torsos, nibbled our swim fins, and played tug-of-war with the Zodiac's lifesaver ring. They are aqua-puppies. On the lava shore of Santiago Island we saw a little fellow who'd just been born. Like a well-bred American Kennel Club dam, his mother allowed us an up-close look. No one asked, "How do they taste?"

At that evening's fantail colloquium, fly-casters asked bird-hunters, "Is there a reason we couldn't train sea lions to flush bonefish in the Florida Keys?"

The adult male sea lions, the bulls, wouldn't be much use. They spend their lives guarding a particular stretch of beach from sea lion pool boys, sea lion UPS drivers, etc. Meanwhile their wives come and go as they please. "I tell my clients," said the Dallas lawyer, "just *give* her the house."

Not that our tour group meant to introduce collars and kennels or animal divorce courts into the Galápagos. There's been enough disturbance of nature's balance. Feral goats, let loose by settlers from the mainland, ate the giant tortoise habitat. On the smaller islands the goats have now cashed in their 401(k)s, but Santiago still has tens of thousands. The Charles Darwin Foundation, the World Wide Fund for Nature, and other organizations are spending millions on goat eradication. We volunteered to do it for free. Well, not exactly for free. But give us the goat-hunting rights and we'd sell trips to the Galápagos to wealthy American sportsmen offering unlimited trophy goat opportunities. The Lindblad people looked dubious.

The Galápagos Islands do need assistance, however. The government of Ecuador does its best but is hampered by being, frankly, the government of Ecuador. Send lawyers, guns, and money. Actually, our group had the lawyers and guns. Send just the money to donations@darwinfoundation. org. Think of those giant tortoises. They date back to the age of the dinosaurs. They have movie-star good looks. (*E.T.* was a huge hit.) And there's something about the giant tortoises that's just so . . . so . . . "Extinctable," said Laura. "When life-forms that had more on the ball than dinosaurs arrived, they thought, 'It comes in its own casserole dish!'"

On Santa Cruz Island we saw a few tortoises in the wild. They're easy enough to find, being in exactly the same place they were when the last Lindblad tour came through. Top speed is approximately zero. And we saw a turtle herd at the Charles Darwin Biological Research Station, where a tortoise dating service is attempting to reestablish various subspecies and repopulate the Galápagos. According to research station literature, "When hormonal levels are running high, male tortoises have even been known to try mounting rocks . . ."

"Ugggh, *men!*" said the women in our group.

"Mating is very vigorous," the research station biologist said. He pointed to the last male of the *pinta* subspecies. "We knew that this one was sexually dysfunctional when he copulated for only twenty minutes."

"Ooooo, *turtles!*" said the women.

And then there is the pure beauty of nature in the Galápagos. One afternoon, steaming between islands, we encountered a pod of 1,000 dolphins, jumping in undulations, Baryshnikoving above the waves. Even the Buchanan Republicans among us held their breath in awe and thereby briefly honored the Kyoto Protocol on climate change. Out beyond the dolphins was a basking sperm whale, such a magnificent creature that, we all concurred, harming it would be as bad as seeing a "SAVE THE WHALES" bumper sticker on your congressman's car.

"This trip really *is* educational," said the Dallas lawyer. "Suddenly I want to read *Moby-Dick,* and not the CliffNotes, either."

"And forty years after the fact, I finally understand my statistics class," said George. He was referring to the penguins and flamingos we'd seen the previous day. This is the only place on earth that has both. The Galápagos are on the equator, so they're tropical, but the icy Humboldt Current cools the air, forming a dense foggy mist called a *garúa* that gets everything cold and soaking wet even though the Galápagos are desert islands. The climate is perfect—if you average it. Confusing "average" with "median," as we all did in statistics class, penguins and flamingos both arrived.

I think we were also supposed to be learning something from the famous Darwin finches. But, to tell the truth, they're small, drab, and boring. It is a mark of Darwin's genius that he noticed them at all. Then, by observing the various evolutionary modifications in their little beaks, Darwin somehow discovered that men are descended from monkeys, although he would have known this already if he'd asked the men's wives.

Which goes to show that not all lessons in ecology are edifying. The marine iguana, for example. Washing ashore from the mainland, it learned to go with the flow. It became the only seagoing lizard. It eats nothing but algae. Here is the lizard version of moving to Humboldt County, California, growing your own vegetables, and weaving your clothes from hemp. Marine iguanas are as dull as folk songs and as ugly as unglazed pottery. They spend all day lying on top of each other in big iguana group gropes.

Looking at the marine iguanas, the Dallas lawyer said to his wife, "Honey, do you think we should have left the teenagers home by themselves?"

2

MONUMENTAL GENERATIONS

The National World War II Memorial, Washington, D.C., June 2004

❖

The World War II Memorial squats on the Mall between the Lincoln Memorial and the Washington Monument. From afar its purpose seems to be to mar the vista. From up close its purpose is less certain.

The Memorial was dedicated on May 29, 2004—something of a tardy homage to the combat veterans of the war, who were by then mostly near eighty or dead. On the other hand, no mere shrine to combat bravery seems to be intended. According to the Web site that all persons, places, and things nowadays must have, "The World War II Memorial honors the sixteen million who served in the armed forces of the U.S., the more than 400,000 who died, and all who supported the war effort from home . . . a monument to the

spirit, sacrifice, and commitment of the American people."
In other words, a monument to showing up.

The Memorial was designed by Friedrich St. Florian,
who, just going by his name, sounds like a fellow that
America has fought a couple of wars against, such as the
French and Indian and World War II. Mr. St. Florian did
his designing in the neoclassic idiom—if the classic or-
ders of architecture are Dorky, Ironic, and Corny-inthian.
A seven-and-a-half-acre plaza is sunk below the ground,
though not nearly far enough.

A pair of ill-proportioned four-story-high open-roofed
structures, which could be construed as chapels if separation
of church and state allowed chapels on the Mall, bookend a
fountain-filled oval fringed with fifty-six bell-less belfries—
one for each state, territory, and miscellaneous American
domain including the Virgin Islands, the Philippines, Puerto
Rico, American Samoa, the District of Columbia, and Guam.
(What, no Canal Zone?) Ask not for whom the imaginary
bell tolls.

I might be wrong about these being bell towers. Maybe
"Croquet Wickets de Triomphe" is the effect being sought.
The two chapels—perhaps they're stone gazebos—have bronze
sculptures where their domes would be if they had domes.
The sculptures, I believe, depict bald eagles getting tangled
in Christmas wreaths. The gazebos are labeled "Atlantic"
and "Pacific," causing anyone remotely close to the age of a
World War II vet to automatically think "Tea Company." The
fountain pools, though lacking fish, are very fish pond–like,
and these, combined with an artificial waterfall, produce a
miniature golf course foreground for the Lincoln Memorial.
A Vegas touch is also provided in a wall of gold stars equal-
ing (by some mathematical ratio that isn't self-evident) the

number of U.S. war dead. Elsewhere are scattered incised quotations of a barely stirring nature:

> Women who stepped up were measured as citizens of the nation, not as women. . . . This was a people's war, and everyone was in it.
>
> —Col. Oveta Culp Hobby

The American Battle Monuments Commission must have looked hard for that one. As to its being a "people's war," had previous wars been fought by furniture, toys, and pets?

The World War II Memorial is entered from the east, down steps to the sunken plaza. Flanking the steps are haut-relief bronze panels sculpted in a style that could be called "accused-of-being-socialist realism." They depict scenes from the Atlantic theater, on the right, and the Pacific theater, on the left. The Pacific tableaux begin with alarmed people listening to the radio (news from Pearl Harbor, one supposes) and end with V-J Day celebrations in Times Square. The Atlantic tableaux begin with an attempt at a visualization of the Lend-Lease Program and end with our GIs shaking hands with Soviets, smiles all around.

This is not a fit monument to the American men who fought the war. But it isn't meant for them, what with their being near eighty and dead and all. The Memorial is, rather, a sentimental gesture toward the whole "Greatest Generation," about whom we are getting so sentimental now that we've put them in nursing homes.

This *is* a fit monument to the American men, women, and politicians who endured a global depression only partly of their own making, struggled to free mankind from totalitarian oppression by fascists and communists (once they'd gotten over admiring the efficiencies of the former and being allies with the latter), and rebuilt the postwar world—with seven-foot ceilings and cheap hollow doors. We call them the Greatest Generation, and we call them other things when we're stuck behind them in the ten-items-or-less grocery store checkout lane while they debate with the clerk about expiration dates on discount coupons for oleomargarine. Their World War II Memorial doesn't quite ruin the Mall.

I am reminded of the 1960s, when my own generation did a much more thoroughgoing job of ruining the Mall during various attempts to end war, expand cosmic consciousness, crush capitalist-pig imperialism, meet girls, and score pot. I can't help wondering when we will get our monument.

Technically, I suppose, the Vietnam Memorial counts. Vietnam veterans were for the most part born in the same years as my friends and I. But those were the kids who when somebody yelled "Get a haircut!" got a haircut—or, anyway, the Army gave them one free. What about *my* part of my generation? What about the Veterans of Domestic Disorders? I know Vietnam was a tough and terrifying experience. But you should have seen the fights around the dinner table at my house. Dad went ballistic when he discovered that I'd joined a commune that was living in the basement rec room. And when the cops broke out the tear gas at the anti-war demonstrations, my friends and I had to tap reserves of strength and will that we didn't know we possessed, to run away as fast as we did.

We cared. My generation of Americans was the first to really care about racism and sexism, not to mention the I Ching, plus, of course, the earth. "It's important to preserve the earth's resources," I remember saying to Windflower, a pert blonde. "You and I will have to double up in the shower to get this tear gas off." Also, we were committed. I recall several people whose families had them committed.

We changed the world. Life has never been the same since that "youthquake" of forty-some years ago. Think of all the things we wouldn't have if not for the uninhibited freedom and creativity of the 1960s: Ben & Jerry's Cherry Garcia ice cream, Narcotics Anonymous twenty-four-hour help lines, Cher, the Volkswagon New Beatle, comedians who use the word "bullshit" on network TV (after ten PM), cats named Chairman Meow, retro 1960's clothing fashions, retro 1960's hairstyles, retro 1960's music fads, herpes.

As a generation, perhaps we weren't the "greatest," but we certainly were the greatest surprise, when we returned from college drenched in patchouli oil, spouting Karl Marx, and wearing clown pants and braids in our beards. Members of the Greatest Generation pride themselves on all the tribulations they survived, but many of them never got over that one. Mercifully, most members of my generation did. It's been said that we never had to make sacrifices. Not true. Lots of us are awake by nine o'clock in the morning and have jobs.

We got married, had families, straightened out, got married again, had more families, straightened out (really). There can be no greater sacrifice than that a man lay down his lifestyle for others. And—"we are all one"— for himself, too, once he figures out that golf is more fun than hacky sack and decides he wants a Lexus. But that doesn't mean I won't pay fifty cents a cup extra to make sure that my coffee has been organically grown and ecologically harvested in a way that does not cause political or economic exploitation.

Speaking of sacrifices, the Veterans of Domestic Disorders Memorial should be engraved with names of those who perished in order that the world might be, you know, groovy. Several prominent rock musicians come to mind, although celebrity drug overdoses could send the wrong message to our own kids who are under the impression that, yes, Dad did have funny hair in the 1960s, but he spent the entire decade singing "Kumbaya" at folk Mass.

There were those poor students who died at Kent State, except I can't remember their names. That's a problem with engraving names on a 1960's monument. What with the ingestion of this and that and people giving themselves monikers like "Windflower," it's hard to remember anyone's name from back then. But this is a detail. The important question is the concept and design of the memorial.

My wife, a member of Generation X (and I'm betting that *their* monument will consist of a Prada backpack with a *Brady Bunch* CD inside), thinks the 1960's memorial should be something that would allow members of my generation to contemplate the driving force behind the era. She suggests a mirror. I'd like it to be slightly concave to produce an image that is slimming. My uncle Mike (Marine Corps, Iwo) proposes a large ditch with a donkey in it, although he puts that in somewhat different words. But the donkey might be misconstrued—many Veterans of Domestic Disorders being, these days, Republicans. A competition should be opened, with invitations extended to the most talented architects and artists born from 1946 to 1964. (No burnouts who live in yurts or belong to crafts collectives, please.) I trust this competition will produce something with dignity, grandeur, and a place to stash a roach if the park police come nosing around.

3

ROUND ON THE ENDS AND "HI!" IN THE MIDDLE

Ohio Skiing, February 2005

❖

Time for a family ski vacation. "How about Gstaad?" said Mrs. O., grabbing a Bogner catalog.

"How about Aspen?" said I, having an inappropriate "single-in-the-1970s" flashback.

"How about Disney World?" said Poppet, age four.

"There's no skiing at Disney World," I said.

"Whatever," said Poppet.

When it's time for a family ski vacation, you have to be honest about your family. Mrs. O. has been on skis about once since our eldest child, Muffin, age seven, made her sonogram debut. "I love skiing," says Mrs. O. And she does, except for getting cold, being outdoors, and sliding around on skis.

"I like the hot chocolate," says Poppet.

And our youngest, Buster, is thirteen months. There are really only two skiers in the family, and only one is any good. I didn't learn to ski until I was thirty. And when and where I learned (see flashback above), the powder was mostly on glass-topped coffee tables and "downhill" was a description of character tendencies.

I have reformed my personal life but not my ski technique. I'm a bunny-slope Sonny Bono. Muffin, on the other hand, was skiing before she could count to her boot size. Her turns and runs are quicker than the French army's. She whips through moguls that give me knee surgery just looking at them. But Muffin has a problem. It's not exactly fear of heights; she takes the most Himalayan chairlift rides as complacently as if she were in a car seat. Rather, she has "ski agoraphobia." When she gets to the top of a hill and sees more than forty-five degrees of the horizon revealed, she defaults into snowplow lockdown and starts missing her mom in the lodge. Muffin hates vistas.

I surveyed our family ski vacation needs: For Muffin, not too much scenery. For the rest, not too much skiing. I peeked into the bank account. Not too much money. I had an inspiration. There's a place that gets snow almost every day of winter, and it has the added advantage that I'm from there.

"Ohio! Hooray!" said Muffin. "Aunt Loulou let my cousin Tiffany get pierced ears in first grade!"

"We are not staying with your relatives," said Mrs. O.

"What's round on the ends and high in the middle?" I quizzed the girls. "O-*hi*-O." They looked puzzled. As well they might, since the maximum elevation in the state is 1,549 feet. Not that the Alpine Valley ski area, east of Cleveland, is anywhere near so dizzying. It has 230 feet of vertical drop. When Muffin and I stood on the peak of Exhibition, Alpine's black diamond, mmm . . . cubic zirconium run, we were pretty much level with the ski lodge's chimney top. I gave Muffin my Ohio avalanche safety lecture: "You are so safe from avalanches." And I told her not to ski out of bounds.

"Why?"

"Because it's completely flat."

I'm almost certain—although I got a D in high school physics—that somebody on stubby super sidecuts with no poles who weighs less than a down comforter is slower than a fifty-seven-year-old wide load on early 1990's Rossignols the length of *War and Peace*. But a view from the summit that was as exciting as standing on a footstool had reassured Muffin. Before I could say, "Follow me and watch how I turn," she was back in the lift line. So I put her in a private lesson. Doubtless there's much I could still teach Muffin, but I'd have to catch her first.

I put Poppet in a lesson as well. Poppet is that child who already knows as much as she cares to know about whatever you want to teach her. "Whatever," in fact, is her particular favorite word. "I know the alphabet—A, B, G, D, whatever."

Alpine Valley's ski school director Rich Cunningham assigned instructor Joe Cooper to deal with whatever, and he put instructor Dave Hall in charge of Muffin. Alpine's marketing director Jodi Tusik found a quiet spot in a function room for Buster and our family babysitter. The babysitter had trepidations about the trip. She comes from a part of the world with indoor temperatures outdoors. But then she realized—what with the jolly bustle in Alpine Valley's lodge and the uncrowded nature of Alpine Valley's slopes—a lot of Ohio skiing is done indoors.

Dave and Joe would return with glowing reports of Muffin's and Poppet's behavior. This leads me to suspect that Dave couldn't catch Muffin either and that Joe was being diplomatic or, as we call it at our house, lying. More to the point, Muffin and Poppet were themselves aglow and full of hints that adoption by the Alpine Valley ski school would be a parental upgrade. I gather Alpine does not use the "damn-it-listen-to-me" instructional method favored by Dad.

Meanwhile, Mrs. O. and I had our first chance to spend the day skiing together since 1997. Being diplomatic, I'd say she was a little rusty. While "damn-it-listen-to-me" may dampen relations with your children, it produces a tsunami in relations with your spouse. A good family ski experience depends on an adept movement with one part of the body. Shutting the mouth.

Once I clammed up, Alpine Valley was a swell family ski area. This was Tuckerman Ravine as far as Poppet was concerned. There was enough challenge for Muffin and little enough worry for her parents. On seventy-two well-supervised acres, Muffin couldn't get much more lost than we want her to be.

The snowboard park was around a corner so Muffin need not see that cousin Tiffany's earrings are the least of Mom's worries in the piercings department. Employees and customers were possessed of a downright, fundamental Red State friendliness as if they were made from John Kerry antimatter. We were happy at Alpine Valley. I can prove it mathematically:

2 adult lift tickets	$52 (and in three years I get the ½-price senior discount)
1 child lift ticket	$24
1 under-6 lift ticket	$ 8
3 equipment rentals	$55
2 private lessons	$64
=	$ Lunch in Vail

You might think Alpine Valley lacked thrills for me. You'd be wrong. There was one run that took my breath away and transported me to that near weightless sense of bliss, a giddy marriage of flight and free fall, where I was beyond command yet not out of control. This was the tube ride I took with Muffin.

The line for the inner tubes was much longer than the lines for the chairlifts. Come to that, so was the line for lunch. Ohio exposes the id of winter sports. Secretly we'd all rather be sitting down.

Ohio's skiers do a lot of their sitting down on the slopes. The Boston Mills ski area is southeast of Cleveland and very similar to Alpine Valley in size, bargain value, solicitousness, and pleasant company. A sunny forty-degree day had brought out large numbers of that pleasant company. Their skiing explained how Ohio has produced seven presidents and no Bode Millers. The problem is one that's not addressed by instruction books, instruction videos, or instructors. Ohioans, with no point of reference for skiing except what they do in the summer at the lake, are trying to water-ski. They carefully distribute their weight on both skis and hunch to compensate for the pulling power of gravity, which they picture as a metaphorical 100-horsepower Evinrude. A special form of Ohio ski teaching is needed. Most Ohioans know how to ice-skate. A video called "Playing Hockey with Planks on

Your Feet" would be invaluable, although this might cause Ohioans to start high-sticking with their poles and thereby spoil the atmosphere at Boston Mills.

Alternatively, Ohioans could spell our babysitter and watch Buster toddle. He does fine as long as he's shifting from foot to foot and maintaining forward progress. But when he tries to plant himself firmly on two feet, he sits down.

Boston Mills' marketing manager Kim Laubenthal helped us sit Buster down with our babysitter in the clean, cheerful cafeteria. Even the undersides of the tables were clean, our babysitter remarked, having seen all of them while chasing Buster. We foisted off Poppet on an amiable certified kids' instructor, Herta Schwaiger. Mrs. O. went to ski somewhere out of the range of advice from me. Or she said she did. (Several malls are nearby.) And I took Muffin on the Boston Mills expert run.

This turned out to *be* an expert run. Or sixty yards of it was. A landfill ramp had been bulldozed out from the modest natural slope of the hill. Beyond the lip of this ramp was the closest thing Ohio has to a headwall. Muffin went right over the edge. My heart pumped, but not as fast as her knees. She went down in half a dozen perfect little parallels with daylight beneath her skis on every one. She did this another fifteen times. It is impossible for a child to be bored by anything that scares a parent.

Alongside the headwall run was a genuine, if abbreviated, mogul field. Here Daddy messed up. I swear I can turn once as well as anyone. It's just that before I can turn again, I—to judge by my mogul performance—need to sit down. Muffin skied the bumps with the special grace of a seven-year-old girl, part ballerina and part frog.

The headwall and mogul field shared a chairlift with the snowboard park. The teenage snowboarders were much better than the adult skiers. Summers on a skateboard give you moves you don't get being dragged behind a Correct Craft. Plus, no Alps or Rockies are needed for snowboarding. You can just neglect to shovel wheelchair access ramps and slide the railings. But these were Ohio snowboarders, with no tattoos. As for piercing, only the high school girls' giggles were that. They were all wearing the requisite bag-it-came-in clothing, but the snowboarder attitude eluded Ohio youngsters. They fussed over Muffin. It will be a shock to the sport when the Greater Cleveland Style hits snowboarding at the X-treme Yes Ma'am No Ma'am games with Hilary Duff blasting from the speakers during the half-pipe competition.

I lured Muffin back to the cafeteria with a promise that she could try snowboarding just as soon as the College of Orthopedic Surgeons and her mom say it is OK. Herta Schwaiger gave an upbeat assessment of Poppet's skiing progress.

"She's very sweet, and she can do almost everything now."

"Everything but stop," said Poppet.

"Well, yes," Herta said, "her stopping needs some work."

"I stopped for hot chocolate," Poppet said.

Mrs. O. returned from skiing suspiciously un-snow-encrusted. Buster was retrieved from under a table. And we all went back to our superluxury spa resort off Interstate 90 in Concord, Ohio.

If you don't think there's a superluxury spa resort off Interstate 90 in Concord, Ohio, it's because you don't travel with three small children and don't know the meaning of superluxury. It means connecting rooms with doors that can be opened only from the parents' side; PBS Kids and no Jerry

Springer on the cable TV; speedy room service specializing in shocking-colored, fudge-flavored breakfast cereals and chicken fingers; patient, forgiving housekeepers who can erect a portable crib and are handy with a mop; and a really shallow indoor pool where air and water temperatures are slightly too high for humans and thus perfect for Muffin, Poppet, and Buster. Of such is the luxury at Renaissance Quail Hollow Resort, which also has a steak house worthy of a state full of cows (serving chicken fingers, too) with patient, forgiving waitresses who are handy with a mop. As for the spa part, a cigar bar serves single-malt Scotch as old as I felt when the kids got their second wind and began doing cordless bungee jumps on the king-size bed.

"Honey," I said to my wife, "I need to go check my e-mail."

"There's no Internet access in the cigar bar," said Mrs. O.

"Whatever."

Ohio provided other, less expected, luxuries. Peter and Paris Ferrante, members of the Cleveland Ski Club, took us to dinner at Ferrante Winery and Ristorante, owned by Peter's family. Ohio has better ethnic food than New York City, for a simple reason. The more enterprising immigrants to America—even the O'Rourkes—realized that Ohio was a better deal than the slums of Manhattan. And one of the first enterprises of the more enterprising immigrants was to fix dinner. There's Cincinnati schnitzel, Cleveland kielbasa, Toledo falafel. Ferrante's food was best of all. The veal dishes would challenge the sincerity of the most rigorous food ethicist. The squid could send Neapolitan fisherman to cast their nets in the Great Lakes. But it was the wine that amazed. Ohio has wine but it's mostly from Concord grapes, the grapes used to make a PB&J. Cork up some of those jelly jars with the Flintstones on them, store these in your basement for a few years, and you've got Ohio wine. The Ferrante family, however, has been working for seventy years to grow grapes for adults on the shores of Lake Erie. The result is that splendid wine you get at a bistro in Italy, the wine that comes to the table in an unmarked carafe, and when you ask what it is, the waiter offers only Mediterranean shrugs and evasions—because it's imported from Ohio.

But does Ohio have skiing that's equally great? Actually, in a way, it does. The Cleveland Ski Club was organized in 1937 and is one of the few ski clubs in America that owns its own hill. Most Ohio skiers are Ohioans stuck on skis. Cleveland Ski Club members are skiers stuck in Ohio. When they can't get to Jackson Hole or Stowe they go thirty miles east of Cleveland to Big Creek. They found the property by looking at topo maps and asking the state highway department where it had the most trouble plowing roads. Big Creek isn't really a hill. The slope goes down, not up, into a 175-foot-deep, heavily wooded gorge. The club hired a timber company to clear four ski trails. Each is a version, in miniature, of a perfect run. A broad, arcing sweeper is smooth enough for childrens' lessons but fast enough to race on, and it provides three minutes of micro-cruising. A wider, precipitous, mildly bumped descent flutters the tummy. Or you can gut-wrench yourself on a more precipitous, ungroomed version where you swallow all 175 feet in one gulp. Then there's a nightmare of a glade, or, if not quite long enough to be a nightmare, a nightmare's coming-attractions reel.

Big Creek is open to the public but seems to be skied usually by club devotees, some of them third-generation members. The club does most of the maintenance and grooming itself. On the lip of the gorge there's a small Swiss-style chalet full of kids, prized chili recipes in potluck dishes, and parents keeping babies from crawling into the fireplace. Outside, the snowbanks are stuck full of cold beers.

Big Creek has two T-bars. Mastering these up the side of the gorge is a better test of skiing skills than conquering the Colorado backcountry. Muffin had a last-moment flinch that sent the T-bar into Dad's kidney. Ski Club kids Poppet's age were unfazed. They made my skiing look like Poppet's.

Lest Poppet end up skiing like me forever, I tried to give her a lesson. I held her under her arms, plopped her into the ample wedge made by my old-fashioned skis, and headed down the sweeper. Apparently Poppet has been studying the techniques of nonviolent protest and passive resistance (perhaps in the works of Gandhi—she attends a progressive preschool). She went completely limp, converting her thirty-five pounds into the stuff at the center of black holes in space. Thank you, Quail Hollow, for the parboil-temperature swimming pool, which makes a petty good whirlpool bath if you put your lower back against the filtration outlet.

Poppet's best winter sport is making snow angels. She does it intentionally if you take off her skis, and I promptly did. Muffin competed in her first ski race. She placed third in her age group. I placed about 281st in mine, the Cleveland Ski Club having 280 members. Poppet made friends with some like-minded little girls and proceeded from intermediate to advanced snow angels. Everybody was looking after everybody's children, so Mrs. O. could go off with Paris Ferrante and other moms. The last I saw of my wife, as she plunged into the gorge, was a pair of skis that had been smartly brought together and the cute little hip thrust she made when she carved her turn. Our babysitter discovered that Ohio chili is spiced to a degree that's alarming even by the standards of her native land. Buster crawled happily into the fireplace. I had a beer. And another.

Go ahead and go to Park City if you're taking a ski vacation. But if you're taking a *family* ski vacation . . . Plus, if Cleveland becomes a winter travel destination, think what an improvement on Sundance its film festival will be. You won't have to sit through any solemn bum-out documentaries or pretentious handheld indie productions or incomprehensible art films—because Drew Carey will be picking all the movies.

4

Riding to the Hounds versus Going to the Dogs

Britain after the Hunting Ban, March 2005

❖

A stag flanked by two female red deer, or "hinds," trotted down a steep moorland pasture toward a wood. Two mounted hunters were behind them, and staghounds were in between. The deer's trot was faster than the hunters' canter and as fast as the all-out run of the hounds. A horn was blown. We were off—over a soaked, slippery sheep meadow, between the stone posts of a narrow gate, down a muddy track perilous with ruts, into a country lane of barely an arm's breadth, through the tiny streets of an old village with tourists hopping out of our way, then making a hairpin turn onto a paved road, speeding uphill around blind curves, and narrowly avoiding several head-on collisions with trucks. It was a thrilling ride, even if it was in a Suzuki SUV driven by a retired grocer, an enthusiast of stag hunting who had volunteered to show me the hunt on Exmoor in England's West Country.

We arrived at a hilltop opposite the steep pasture and above the woods. From here I could look across a valley at . . . not much. On the crest of the far slope several dozen members of the hunt were sitting on their horses. They watched two dogs sniffing the underbrush below. Two men in scarlet coats were with the dogs, more closely watching them sniff.

The idea of a stag hunt evokes chivalry—knights in jerkins and hose, ladies on sidesaddles with wimples and billowing dresses, a white stag symbolizing something or other, and Robin Hood getting in the way. An actual stag hunt is more like a horseback meeting of a county planning commission. The equestrian committee is responding to deer-population-growth issues and deer-herd rural sprawl. Red deer are noble animals—big, anyway. They are half again the size of American whitetails. In the fall a mature stag has antlers that could hang the hats of a small town in Texas. But red deer are also pests. England is intensely cultivated. A farmer may find a hundred red deer in his pasture, each eating as much grass as three sheep. The deer's zoning permits are revoked by a process too deeply imbued with tradition to be called bureaucratic, but which is a reminder that one of civilization's oldest traditions is bureaucracy. Stag hunts cull the weaker hinds from November through February, the less promising young stags in hunts such as this one in March, and the stags whose days of promise are behind them during late summer and fall.

Each hunt has a "harbourer," a specialist whose job is to watch the herds and select a specific stag. Only this one is to be hunted. (When hunting hinds, which are effectively indistinguishable, the selection is made by the hounds on Darwinian principles. Thus there is an intellectual connection between the British ban on hunting with dogs and the American call for teaching creationism in schools.)

A chivalrous aspect to stag hunting remains, however. The three hunts in the Exmoor region maintain, with noblesse oblige, a twenty-four-hour emergency service for sick or injured deer. Mostly these are deer that have been hit by cars and have crawled off into the bushes—as many as a hundred of them a year. Members of the hunts will come out in the middle of the night with horses and dogs, to track these suffering creatures. In some years the hunters do as much euthanizing as they do hunting.

For a proper hunt, or "meet," in which Rovers and BMWs do not initiate the pursuit, the harbourer spends the previous day and night making sure of the stag's location. On the morning of the hunt he reports to his chief, the huntsman. The huntsman brings in older, experienced hounds, called "tufters," to separate the stag from the herd. It was this singling-out that I was watching in the steep moorland pasture. But it hadn't been working perfectly. As unpromising as that young stag may have been from the harbourer's point of view, the two hinds thought he was worth running away with. Once the stag is solitary, the huntsman's assistant, the "whipper-in," is supposed to bring up the full pack, and the hunt's members and guests fall in behind the hounds. Miles and miles of furiously galloping cross-country endeavor at achievement of ecological balance in the Exmoor deer herds ensues. Unless it doesn't. As it seemed not to be doing from my vantage point across the valley. When the chase does happen, the usual outcome is that the stag, at last, turns and "stands at bay," facing the hounds. Then (rather disappointingly for those whose imaginations run to tenderhearted indignation or to bloodlust) the hounds do not tear the stag to shreds. They bark.

There's probably not much else they could do with an irked and antler-waving stag. Staghounds are not giant Scottish deerhounds or hulking, red-eyed mastiffs. They're just foxhounds, happy and hound-doggy and friendly if you aren't prey. "You can set your baby down in the middle of a pack," a hunter told me, "and they'll lick him silly." What happens to the stag is that the huntsman walks over to it and prosaically shoots it in the head with a special, short-barreled, folding-stock shotgun. This is an illegal weapon in Great Britain. But on stag hunts it's legally required.

Speaking of Britain's laws, killing wild mammals with the aid of dogs, as the Exmoor hunt was trying to do, is forbidden. Except when—as I understand the parliamentary Hunting Act of 2004—it is mandatory. The act contains certain conditions for "exempt hunting" that allow the killing of wild mammals with the aid of dogs if "as soon as possible after being found or flushed out the wild mammal is shot dead by a competent person." No letting it go, even if it's Bambi's mother. Furthermore only two dogs may be used at a time. And no letting the dogs kill the wild mammals, the way foxhunters always have done. The stain must be upon you, not your pet. "Out, damned spot," indeed.

The Hunting Act came into effect on February 18, 2005, a few weeks before this Exmoor meet. I got in touch with Adrian Dangar, the hunting correspondent for *The Field*. Adrian said that I shouldn't write about foxhunting. It's all that anybody was writing about. And it's such a social occasion. He said that the stag hunters were a much more doughty and resolute lot, and stag hunting was more of a way of life.

I went to Exmoor with Adrian. We stayed with the chairman of the stag hunt. I'll call him Michael Thompson. He was doughty and resolute, the owner of a family sheep farm of centuries' standing. I went to the meet expecting a scene of American seething, full of the half-suppressed violence that Americans thwarted in their beliefs or their hobbies half-suppress so well. What I found was a cheerful, natty crowd on horseback, booted and spurred and listening to a talk from the hunt secretary about strict adherence to the Hunt Act, especially in the matter of using just two dogs. The whole staghound pack was there, but the hounds had been split into pairs, with each twosome in the back of a different vehicle. The hunt secretary gave her opinion that hunting the pairs serially was in accord with the letter and spirit of the law.

Having just two dogs in the field was exactly the problem. So I was told by the retired grocer and other hunt followers gathered on the hilltop vantage point, watching the lack of action through binoculars. Two hounds were not enough to break the stag away from the hinds. Or two hounds were not enough to bring the stag to bay. Two hounds were certainly not enough to make what I was told was the music of a pack in full cry.

The followers were local farmers and farm wives, mostly past middle age. Many had ridden with the hunt years before. The men wore tweed jackets and neckties. The women wore tweed skirts and twinsets. Everyone wore a waxed cotton Barbour jacket. The hunt members were dressed in black and brown riding coats, buff whipcord breeches, and hunting bowlers. They wore elaborately tied and gold-pinned white stocks at their throats. All the clothes were seasoned and washed to a perfect Ralph Lauren degree. If hunting dies out, from where will Ralph draw outdoorsy English inspiration? Will suburban Americans be wearing the undershirts, rolled trousers, and hankies-on-the-head of English sunbathers?

The hunt was moving. Horses were trotting over the far hill. The two hounds did their best in the music department. There was a spate of elderly, excited driving as hunt followers hurried to find a better view. We parked by a tributary of the River Exe. The stag either did or didn't go into a strip of woods along the bank. The hounds weren't sure. The followers weren't sure. Possibly the stag came out of the woods. Possibly he didn't. The hunters went into the woods and came out. This sounds as interesting as cricket. And to the onlookers it was. The crowd had grown to forty or more and now included children in small tweeds and small Barbour coats and a man selling tea and sandwiches from a van. They all watched intently, the tea vendor included. There was a tense murmuring, as from a golf gallery.

The staghounds and stag hunters trotted through a farmyard, and I followed on foot. Some local farmers are not hospitable to the traffic through their property—not hospitable, specifically, to the traffic of me. I was trying to take notes and make haste and avoid deep puddles and horse droppings, and I wasn't wearing a necktie. "Is he all right?" I heard a farmer ask.

"He thought you were an 'anti,'" the retired grocer explained later. "They come around bothering the hunts."

According to a brochure from the League Against Cruel Sports, "The League . . . has collected an enormous amount of evidence of the cruelty of hunting. Years of undercover work and hunt monitoring has enabled [members of Parliament] to see the real face of hunting."

Beyond the farm, on the Exmoor upland, the real face of hunting was soaking wet. The scenery was an alluring frustration: heather-covered bosomy hill mounds rising above dark nests of woods. A green girlfriend of a landscape. But somebody else's girlfriend, greeting the hunt with cold drizzle and sharp wind.

This buoyed everyone's spirits. The British manner of cheerfully not complaining can't be maintained when there's nothing to cheerfully not complain about. Forty horses ran across the moor. Stag hunting is not as show-offy as foxhunting. There's no jumping of ditches, hedges, and gates. Exmoor is wet through like a bath sponge; no use ditching it for drainage. The hedges are as high as tennis backboards and grow from stone heaps piled up since Roman times. And the farmers leave the gates open because some things are more important than keeping sheep in. I witnessed none of the hat-losing, horse-flipping spectacles seen in engravings on the walls of steak houses. And to be truthful, my entire knowledge of hunting on horseback has been gained by staring at such decor between courses. What sort of engravings will steak houses hang on the paneling a hundred years hence? Pictures of people in Pilates classes?

The excitement in stag hunting comes from the treacherous footing on the soaked, peat-slick moors and from the great length of the stag chase and the great speed of the stag's run. It can also be dangerous just sitting on a horse. A young woman fell off while the hunt was gathered by the riverbank. A medical evacuation helicopter was called. The hunt was uninterrupted.

The Exmoor stag hunters distribute a brochure, in Q&A form, arguing that stag hunting is not particularly inhumane. "Hunters" might well be substituted for "deer."

Q. But deer must be terrified by stag hunting!

A. . . . Deer pay no more heed . . . than a grazing wildebeest (so often seen on TV) does to a pride of lions lunching off a mate nearby.

I had been offered a tame mount on which to follow the hunt.

"How tame?" I asked.

"Very tame."

"There was," I said, "a man who used to come through my neighborhood in the 1950s with a pony and a camera . . ."

"Not that tame."

But I was inspired, watching the hunters dash around on the moor. The horses were beautiful, as tall as those that pull wagons in beer commercials but as gracefully made as what I'd lost fifty dollars on in last year's Kentucky Derby. I vowed to learn to ride—as soon as they got the middle part of horses to be lower to the ground and had the saddles made by BarcaLounger.

Wind, rain, and temperature grew worse. The hunt descended into a precipitous dell where I'd have thought the riders would have to walk their mounts. They didn't. But I couldn't even walk myself. I returned to where the hunt followers were gathered by the side of a road. The followers were disturbed. A pale and agitated young couple were walking down the road. Surely these were "antis." They were dressed head to toe in black.

But the boy and the girl were just lost backpackers who'd made the mistake of going out into nature for fun. The entertainments of nature are of a sterner kind. They were wet and miserable. The hunters were not, or didn't feel that they were. But the stag and every trace of it had vanished, and the hunters decided to "pack it in, to spare the horses."

Michael, Adrian, and I headed back to Michael's farm in his horse van, a bit disappointed. And then through the van windows came that music I'd been told about: the full cry of a pack. It is a bouillabaisse of a noise, with something in it of happy kids on a playground, honking geese headed for your decoys, and the *wheee* of a deep-sea fishing reel when you've hooked something huge. This particular music was being sung soprano. A beagle pack, thirty-some strong, was bounding across a pasture. We got out and hurried in the direction of the chase. Beagling is like foxhunting or stag hunting except that the quarry is hare, and it's done without benefit of horses. Beaglers follow the pack—at a very brisk pace—on foot. Hunting hares with beagles is banned by the Hunting Act. But rabbits can still be hunted. "Because they're considered pests," Michael said. "Because of lot of Labour voters hunt rabbits," Adrian said. Also, for some reason, "the hunting of a hare which has been shot," is permitted.

The pack arced away from us across a broad field. Just as it did, the hare that the beagles weren't supposed to be hunting came at the three of us with a speed hardly credible in a land animal. If it had been less nimble (and bigger) it would have bowled us over. The dogs seemed to have lost the scent.

"The hare went that way!" Michael shouted to the master of the beagle hounds.

"The *shot* hare!" Adrian shouted.

"You mean the 'bush rabbit'!" the master shouted back. Interesting to wonder how many of the MPs voting for the Hunting Act would know a rabbit from a hare if it turned up in their Easter basket. Maybe on a menu.

We spent an hour with the beagles. They no more got a bush rabbit than Michael and Adrian had got a stag, but the clambering and clamor of the beagles were a joy. I'm a strong advocate for animal rights. I am an animal. I belong to Animal NATO—us, dogs, horses (cats are France). And I belong to Animal WTO. We export feed to sheep, cows, pigs, and chickens, and, to maintain the balance of trade, we eat them.

The Thompsons gave a dinner that night. Their house was of *Middlemarch* era but with fewer old bores writing the *Key to All Mythologies,* and more stag heads on the walls. The main course was pork roast from a farm pig, rather than venison from the Exmoor stag (which in any case would have needed to hang for a week). Miscellaneous small terriers sat on guests' laps.

The consensus of the party was that the hunting ban had to do less with loving animals than with bullying people. This was not a class struggle, I was told. The working class was all for hunting, said one guest. And she was a Labour peer. Nor was it, she said (she herself proved the point) a Labour-Tory conflict. Instead, all agreed, a certain kind of today's urban elite was getting its own back at what they saw as a traditional elite that had no use, as Michael Thompson put it, for people "with shaved heads and five earrings and their husbands just as bad." But, all agreed again, hunts aren't as posh as they used to be—and they never were.

There's truth to this, judging from the foxhunting prose laureate R. S. Surtees, who had his h-dropping London shopkeeper Jorrocks hunting with passion in the 1830s. Anthony Trollope wrote, "Surely no man has labored at it as I have done, or hunted under such drawbacks as to distances, money, and natural disadvantages. I am very heavy, very blind. . . . Nor have I ever been in truth a good horseman. . . . But it has been for more than thirty years a duty to me to ride to hounds."

The word "duty" must seem strange to people not involved in field sports, to today's urban elites who don't see the look on the dog's face when the laptop instead of the gun cabinet is opened during bird season. Of course it's tempting to think that the word "duty" always seems strange to modern urban elites.

Still, in a way, the bullies are understandable. There's a certain satisfaction in taking something away from people perceived as having been too certain and self-confident for too long, people who've dominated society but whose dominance is slipping away. Network news anchors come to mind.

Then again, the bullies aren't understandable. Adrian used to be the master of foxhounds for a hunt in northern England. At the annual hunt ball antis protested outside. "With balaclavas pulled down like the IRA," said Adrian. "One told me, 'We'll smash up your car tonight, Adrian.' They knew me by name. They didn't smash my car. They broke every window in my house. I found my dog and her litter of pups covered in shards of glass."

Several of the other guests hunted foxes as well as stags. This was Thursday night. There was a big fox hunt on Saturday, and Sunday was Easter. Conversation turned to how to get Easter shopping done. Shopping on Good Friday was a bit inappropriate, wasn't it? (There are no atheists in fox hunts.)

The fox hunts were doing all right since the hunting ban. They'd taken up "drag hunting." Someone rides ahead pulling cloth soaked in fox scent behind him. The hounds and the hunters follow his course. And if an actual fox pops up along the way . . . well, who can blame the dogs? Ninety-one foxes were killed on the first day of the hunting ban. But what will the country pub of the future be named? "The Something That Smells Like a Fox and Hounds"?

Did the antis have, I asked, any moral point? Yes, a great point—of moral vanity. God didn't make the world good enough for them. Cheese was served. Port was passed. Adrian quoted Surtees: "It's the sport of kings, the image of war without its guilt, and only five-and-twenty percent its danger."

In a nearly identical cultivated, sonorous voice Michael Hobday, spokesman for the League Against Cruel Sports, answered my questions a week later in London. The League Against Cruel Sports was founded in 1924, with antecedents dating to Hogarth's *The Four Stages of Cruelty*. Here are a few of the League's past presidents: Edith Sitwell, Lord Grey de Ruthyn, the Rt. Hon. Earl of Listowel, the Reverend Lord Soper. And a brochure published by the League shows how long and deep is the controversy in Britain about man and his relationship with the animals that are his friends, his relatives, and his dinner. In 1822 Britain passed a law against improper treatment of cattle, the first animal-welfare legislation in history. In 1835 Britain outlawed dogfighting, cockfighting, and bull, bear, and badger baiting. In 1929 the Labour Party adopted a platform plank opposing blood sports (although it held four parliamentary majorities before it fulfilled that campaign promise). "There's a long history of criticism of hunting," Mr. Hobday said. "The people who established the League Against Cruel Sports had a background in the humanitarian movement—animal suffering, welfare of children, prohibition."

I didn't ask if the humanitarian movement had trouble prioritizing. I did ask, "Why the focus on hunting rather than, say, factory farming, with its animal penitentiaries?"

"The reasons are twofold," Mr. Hobday said. "Firstly, foxhunting is an emotive issue. The sight of the blood and gore tugs at the heartstrings. It makes powerful television. Secondly," Mr. Hobday said, "hunting is done for entertainment. It's a sport."

I asked why the law permitted hunting rabbits but not hares.

"The League's view is that cruelty to any animal in the name of sport is wrong. Parliament's view was to make a distinction between activities that were 'necessary' and activities that were undertaken for sport. The Countryside Alliance has a vested interest in pointing out loopholes."

The Countryside Alliance is the principal British prohunting group. Apparently both the League and the Alliance enjoy majority support among the British public. According to a 1997 Gallup poll for *The Daily Telegraph*, 80 percent of Britons disapproved of hunting foxes with hounds. According to a 2004 ICM poll for *The Sunday Telegraph*, 70 percent of Britons believed the police should not enforce the hunting ban.

I wanted to know why hunting (that is, chasing animals with dogs) was banned but shooting (pointing or flushing animals with dogs) wasn't.

"With shooting," Mr. Hobday said, "there are clear steps that people can take to minimize suffering."

Being a better shot was the only one I could think of, and I've been trying for forty years to no avail.

"Using a pack of dogs," Mr. Hobday continued, "with the best will in the world you can't do much about the cruelty. And in practical terms it's impossible to have legislation that covers everything."

I asked if class conflict was involved in the hunting ban.

"From our perspective," Mr. Hobday said, "there's no class element at all. Hare coursing is banned, though it's working class." (Hare coursing is letting greyhounds chase hares in a field—a sort of libertarian dog racing without the bother of a track.) "In the minds of ordinary people," Mr. Hobday said, hunting is "not an issue of class but an issue of behavior. Hunters are seen to behave in a very arrogant fashion—hunts going through smallholdings and gardens. Hunters are very poor about apologizing. There's an attitude of entitlement by hunters: 'It's our land and we have the right.'"

And that, in America, would be all the apologizing needed. I mentioned how different America was—how Senator Kerry hadn't been able to get through his presidential campaign without going on a goose hunt, so there'd be a photo of him holding a gun.

"But not a goose," Mr. Hobday said.

Mr. Hobday told me an anecdote, though he said he couldn't vouch for it personally. Someone on the League's staff had told it to him. At a protest against foxhunting, before the ban, one of the protesters had gone up to a hunter and said, "We're going to make what you do illegal."

The hunter looked down from his horse and said, "People like you obey the law. People like us *make* the law."

This is an anecdote contradicted by what I saw in Exmoor, and exactly opposite to what has happened legislatively, but it still makes good telling. If you understand it, you may understand what's going on in Britain. I don't.

I walked from the offices of the League Against Cruel Sports, in Southwark, to the nearby Tate Modern, to look at the works of Damien Hirst. He is the artist who has floated a sheep in formaldehyde and sliced a cow into sections and so forth for the sake of sculpture. He is today's urban-elite kind of artist—cutting edge, one might say. Unfortunately, the Tate Modern had only one piece by Hirst on display: some seashells with a curator's commentary on the wall beside them:

> "You kill things to look at them," Hirst has said. In this work he arranges a selection of ornate shells, purchased in Thailand, inside a glass cabinet. Resembling a museum display case [for Pete's sake, it *was* a museum display case], it alludes to the 19th century tradition of collecting and classifying natural specimens. Inevitably, the approach involves removing plants and animals from their natural habitats, killing them in order to preserve them . . .

But Hirst was not buying seashells for sport.

In the grassy median of Park Lane, near Hyde Park Speakers' Corner, is the Animals in War memorial—"Unveiled 24 November 2004 by Princess Anne." Its two sweeping curves of concrete wall resemble parts of a non-Euclidian traffic barrier. On the inside of one curve is carved THEY HAD NO CHOICE. Bronze pack mules march toward the gap between the walls. Beyond the gap a bronze dog and a bronze horse walk away, metaphorically in heaven, though actually farther up Park Lane. A eulogy mentions even pigeons. No need to cast one in bronze, though, with so many live ones alighting on the monument.

Here are some British newspaper items I collected on my visit:

> A leading cancer charity has rejected a £30,000 donation from the organizer of sponsored bird shoots because it does not approve of the way the money was raised.
> —*The Sunday Telegraph*, March 20

> Professor John Webster, emeritus professor at Bristol University, discussed the intelligence of chickens at a conference organized by Compassion in World Farming. . . . They are intelligent, sensitive characters.
> —*The Times*, March 31

> Nine New Forest firefighters were involved in freeing a frog from the spout of a watering can. A gardener took the trapped frog to the fire station. . . . It was released after half an hour's vigorous cutting with a hacksaw.
> —*The Times*, March 28

As for the well-being of people:

> A middle-aged teacher is starting a six-month jail sentence today because she decided to fight back against "yobs" with a pellet gun. Linda Walker, 47, . . . was being driven towards breaking point by groups of youth "terrorizing" her neighborhood. . . . She rushed out of her house at night to confront a knot of teenagers. . . . After an exchange of abuse . . . Mrs. Walker squared up to one 18-year-old, firing off several rounds from the [compressed air-powered] pistol into nearby

ground. . . . Mrs. Walker was found guilty of affray and pos-
sessing a firearm with intent to cause fear of violence.
—*The Times*, March 30

Of course, there's always the possibility that barmy Britannia
—or a certain political part of her—is crazy like a . . .

The more aspects of life that can be moved from private
reign to public realm, the better it is for politics. Politicians
don't exactly want to ban hunting or forbid shooting teen
goons with BBs. Politicians just want to turn everything, right
down to what the dog chases, into a political matter. And
they've succeeded. The day I arrived in Britain Tony Blair
was beginning his run for reelection. The campaign issue
making headlines was school lunch menus.

Ordinary people have ordinary knowledge: how to make
things (including lunch), grow things, fix things, build things,
and, for that matter, kill things. Politicians have extraordinary knowledge: how all things ought to be. Never mind
that politicians do not, as it were, run with the hare *or* hunt
with the hounds.

All things ought to be, as far as I'm concerned, the way
they were on Michael Thompson's farm. When the dinner
after the stag hunt was over, at one in the morning, Michael
got up from the table and said, "I'm going to change my
trousers and have a look at the lambing."

More than a thousand of his ewes were giving or about
to give birth. A vet comes with a portable machine and gives
them sonograms—better service than yuppie moms get. If
a ewe is having one lamb, she can be left on her own in the
fields. But twins can confuse a ewe, especially if it's her first

lambing. She may not know if both or either is hers. Michael went into a shed the size of a modest railroad station, where hundreds of sheep were in twenty or so pens. Then he climbed onto a wooden railing separating two banks of pens and, though he is seventy and had done as much justice to the wine at dinner as I had, walked the rail's length looking for newborns. When he spotted a pair, Michael would jump among the sheep, hoist each lamb by a leg, and begin backing toward the pen's gate. This would cause at first a few, then a couple, then, usually, just one of the ewes to follow him—the others dropping back with, frankly, sheepish looks as they (I guess) realized they hadn't had any lambs yet. Then mother and children were put in a stall to bond.

The lambs were still damp from birth, making their first steps, quad-toddling with each little hoof boxing the compass. They were adorable. Also, rather frequently, they were dead. Scores of dead lambs lay in the aisle of the lambing shed, nature being profligate with adorability. As man is. The living lambs would be dead soon enough. Delicious, too.

Tempting to meditate on how vivid and real the lambing was compared with politics. Except that Michael's farm is itself a political construct. Sheep farming is heavily subsidized in Great Britain. Without the subsidies the green grazing in the valley of the River Exe would be gone. The handsome agricultural landscape of which the British are so proud, carefully husbanded since Boudicca's day, would be replaced by natural growth. The most likely growth is real estate developments. There's room for any number of charming weekend getaway homes where the tired politicians of London could get some relaxation and perhaps provide their constituents with a bit of sport—of a noncontroversial kind. According to the Hunting Act, "The hunting of rats is exempt."

5

My EU Vacation

*Reading the European Constitution on a
French Beach, Guadeloupe, May 2005*

❖

The French referendum on the EU Constitution was a story
that demanded to be viewed and understood from a thor-
oughly European perspective, so I went on vacation.

Guadeloupe is a full-fledged *département* of metropolitan
France. Here the European Union could be contemplated
as the sociopolitico-economic masterwork of a civilization,
an edifice of human hope. And never mind that previous
attempts to unify Europe by Hitler, Napoleon, and Attila
the Hun didn't work out—it had been a cold, rainy spring
in New England.

At passport control there were two lines. One official
sat complacently in a booth doing nothing until all the EU
citizens had been processed at another booth by a second

official, who, in reciprocation, sat complacently doing nothing while the first official took his turn. When, at last, the first official deigned to examine a non-EU passport he walked across the aisle to the second official's booth, borrowed the visa stamp, walked back, stamped the passport, and returned the stamp to his colleague. He did the same thing for each subsequent passport. At customs, on the other hand, there were no officials.

All around the island billboards read "OUI" or "NON." They were equal in number and identical in color and typography. The fairness doctrine debates of the U.S. election must have hit home in the EU. Obviously rigorous, uniform rules on campaign media had been instituted. I mentally composed several indignant paragraphs about how John McCain will be advocating this soon in the United States before I noticed that the billboards were advertising a cell phone company. Say "NON" to service charges, "OUI" to free minutes.

Real pro and con referendum posters had to be looked for. They were on special hoardings outside schools and municipal offices where the pasting up of expressions of free speech was officially sanctioned. Campaign rhetoric had a certain subtle European sophistication. At least I guess so. The slogan on one "Oui" poster was "*L'Europe—à besoin de notre.*" According to the dictionary I bought for high school French, this translates as "The Europe—to, at, in, on, by, or for need, want, or necessity of ours."

Guadeloupe is a volcanic island of soaring, majestic beauty upon which the French have turned their backs to build everything as close as possible to the damp-spritzed, wind-butted beaches with sand the color of Hyundai fake wood trim and a profusion of foot-piercing volcanic rocks. Also, what's French for "Every litter bit hurts"? Some of the older buildings have a limbo-party-at-the-Phi-Delt-house charm. They will be torn down as soon as the French economy finally revives and more reinforced concrete is poured in the European Bauhaus style. Form follows function. The function is to grow tropical mold.

That said, Guadeloupe's main city, Pointe-à-Pitre, is nice enough, with no glaring slums, no glaring locals, and only the Caribbean minimum of starving stray dogs. Plenty of new Citroëns, Peugeots, and Renaults grace the traffic jams, although Guadeloupe's per capita GDP is only $8,000. The people are sleek and fashionably dressed. The streets are well-swept by the standards of the tropics and well-paved by the standards of New York. Some gang graffiti are visible but only in easily reached places where paint can be sprayed without ruining school clothes. Guadeloupe seems like a swell place to be poor—if poor is what you like to be.

Perhaps the benign and comfortable atmosphere is a result of French culture and values, such as those the French imparted to Haiti. More likely it's the result of the large subsidies evident in the excellent road system that extends to every place on the island including places no one goes. And Guadeloupe has more impressive government buildings than an overseas *département* with a population of 450,000 could need, enough for a minor European country (which France, now that it's rejected the EU Constitution, has arguably become).

As beach reading that constitution fulfills one criterion— it's 485 pages long. And Danielle Steele could not worsen the prose style: "The institutions of the Union shall apply the principle of subsidiarity as laid down in the Protocol on the application of the principles of subsidiarity and proportionality." Every aspect of European life is considered in exquisite detail; vide Annex I, pages 403 and 404, clarifying agricultural trade regulations for "edible meat offal" and "lard and other rendered pig fat."

I slathered myself, instead, in Bain de Soleil and spread my towel between pumice and discarded Gauloises packs. Timing ten pages of attentive reading, I calculated that it would take seventeen hours and three minutes to peruse the full document, by which time I should be quite tan.

According to its constitution, the EU is (or was) to have five branches of government: the European Parliament, the European Council, the Council of Ministers, the European Commission, and the Court of Justice of the European Union; plus two advisory bodies: the Committee of the Regions and the Economic and Social Committee; and four additional independent institutions: the European Central Bank, the European Investment Bank, the Court of Auditors, and the European Ombudsman. Here we have a system of bounced checks and vaudeville balancing acts.

Part II of the constitution, "The Charter of Fundamental Rights of the Union," gives us an idea of what "rights" are supposed to mean in Europe: "Everyone has the right to life." This, on a continent where there's more respect for Dick Cheney than for a fetus. The charter prohibits "making the human body and its parts as such a source of financial gain." No more French actresses showing their tits on the movie screen, and Botox injections will be available only through National Health. There is a "right" to "an annual period of paid leave." (I was having mine.) And a declaration that "The use of property may be regulated by law insofar as is necessary for the general interest." Lenin couldn't have put it better. What there was in this constitution that a subtle, sophisticated European could object to eluded me, as did reading the rest of it.

I was getting bored. I could go hiking in the mountains, except it was ninety-five degrees. I could take a refreshing dip, except the ocean was ninety-five degrees. Guadeloupe's painters and artisans are almost bad enough to get into the Venice Biennale. There was nothing in the stores but European stuff at European prices, and, anyway, the stores were, in European fashion, closed most of the time. I began to get American thoughts about Jet Skis, water park slides, and vast air-conditioned malls. Guadeloupe is lovely. But there isn't much to do except eat. Every third building seems to be a restaurant. I chose one of the most prepossessing establishments. The Big Mac was delicious.

For some reason (and judging by the EU Constitution, it was an elaborate one) the referendum in Guadeloupe was held a day before the referendum in mainland France. I went to a polling place at a reinforced concrete school where "*Joyeux Noël*" decorations still hung in the corridor, and interviewed . . . somebody. She seemed to be in charge of something. I said, "*Parlez-vous* English?"

She said, "*Non.*"

Actually, I claim that there's a tremendous journalistic advantage to covering politics when you can't speak the language. You aren't misled into reporting what people say; you're forced to report the inexorable truth of what people do.

The people of Guadeloupe weren't doing much. They certainly weren't voting. I counted ten voters in the *Joyeux Noël* school and none at the next two polling places I visited. The streets of Pointe-à-Pitre were crowded. The stores were open for a change, but the crowds seemed to be standing around more than shopping. Of course maybe they were standing in line. Guadeloupe provides a very European level of service.

The next day, back in Europe itself, France rejected the EU Constitution because (CNN International informed me) the French were worried about competition from eastern Europeans for French jobs. According to French unemployment figures, the French don't have jobs. In Guadeloupe they're more self-confident about doing nothing. The *département* voted "Oui" in the referendum, albeit with a do-nothing 22 percent turnout.

At the airport, leaving Guadeloupe, I talked to a mainland Frenchman, Antoine. We were standing in line. A reggae band was on our flight. The band had drums. Detailed consideration of the weight and measurements of the drum set had brought seat selection and baggage checking to a halt. Antoine went to buy a bottle of rum and came back twenty minutes later. "This island!" he said. "The airport is full of people and every duty-free shop is closed." Our line hadn't budged. "I have a business friend who lives here," Antoine said. "He was in a line like this at the post office in Pointe-à-Pitre. No one advanced in the line for more than an hour. At last he went to the front of the line and said to the postal clerk, 'Nobody is moving here!' She said, 'Oh, no?' and put up a sign that said 'Out to lunch,' and left."

The French are well advised to worry about competition. But not from the Czechs and Poles. Some citizens of their own country are better at being European than they are.

6

On First Looking into the Airbus A380
Toulouse, June 2005

Sometimes it seems that the aim of modernity is to flush the romance out of life. The library, with its Daedalian labyrinth, mysterious hush, and faintly ominous aroma of knowledge, has been replaced by the computer's cheap glow, pesky chirp, and data spillage. Who born since 1960 has any notion of the Near East's exotic charms? Whence the Rubáiyát? Whither Scheherazade? The Thief of Baghdad is jailed, eating Doritos in his underwear while he awaits hanging. As for romance itself . . . "Had we but world enough, and pills, / For erectile dysfunction's ills." And nothing is more modern than air travel.

As a stimulating adventure, flying nowadays ranks somewhere between appearing in traffic court and going to

Blockbuster with the DVD of *Shrek 2* that my toddler inserted in the toaster. Thus the April 27, 2005, maiden flight of the Airbus A380, the world's largest airliner, did not spark the world's imagination. Or it did—with mental images of a boarding process like going from Manhattan to the Hamptons on a summer Friday, except by foot with carry-on baggage. This to get a seat more uncomfortable than an aluminum beach chair.

What a poor, dull response to a miracle of engineering! The A380 is a Lourdes apparition at the departure ramp. Consider just two of its marvels: Its take-off weight is 1,235,000 pounds. And it takes off. The A380 is the heaviest airplane ever flown, 171 tons heavier than the previous record holder, the somewhat less miraculously engineered Russian Antonov An-124.

A million-and-a-quarter-plus pounds is roughly the heft of 275 full-size SUVs. And, at approximately 90.5 miles per gallon per passenger, the A380 gets much better mileage than my Chevrolet Suburban unless I have a lot of people crammed together in the rear seats (as the A380 doubtless will).

The A380 can fly as fast as a Boeing 747-400 and farther, and the twin passenger decks running the full length of the its fuselage give it half again more cabin space. However, the only expressions of awe about the A380 that I've heard have been awful predictions of the crowd inside. These tend to be somewhat exaggerated. "Oh, my God. Southwest to Tampa with a thousand people!" said a member of my immediate family who often shepherds kids to Grandma's on budget carriers while their dad has to take an earlier flight "for business reasons."

Airbus maintains that with its recommended seating configuration the A380 will hold 555 passengers, versus about 412 in a 747-400. The U.S. House of Representatives, the Senate, the president, the vice president, the cabinet, two swing-voting Supreme Court justices, and Rush Limbaugh can all fly together in an A380. (And maybe *that* statistic will create some popular excitement, if they fly far enough away.) But the London *Sunday Times* has reported that Emirates, an airline with forty-five of the new planes on order, "would pack as many as 649 passengers into the A380." The president of Emirates, Tim Clark, told *The Times*, "Personally, I'd have liked to put 720 seats in." And the chairman of Atlantic Virgin Airways, Sir Richard Branson, has bragged that each Virgin A380 will have a beauty parlor, a gym, double beds, and a casino—three out of four of which sound worse than 719 seatmates.

The headline of *The Times* piece—"New Airbus, Same Old Crush?"—captured the tone of the, to use the mot juste, pedestrian A380 media coverage. Reporters devoted themselves to city sewer commission–style articles considering which tarmacs at what airports could accommodate the A380 and how much gate modifications would cost. Would hub-to-hub markets grow, favoring Europe's Airbus consortium with its A380 capacity maximization? Or was the profit center of the future in destination-to-destination thinking, making the American Boeing corporation's smaller but farther-flying 787 Dreamliner the wise investment choice? As if I were going to buy one of these things.

Airbus itself, in its own promotional literature, did not help. A 302-page corporate publication—"Airbus A380: A New Dimension in Air Travel"—contained such drably titled articles as "Airports Need to Optimise"; "A Vision of the 21st Century" (subtitled "The Future: Forget Speed, Enjoy the Armrests"); and "Airlines Need to Find a New Way," which began:

Aviation has lost its glamour. On the one hand, progress is now measured by sophisticated ratios that make it abstract and no longer the subject of dreams. On the other, air transport has become a commodity. . . . Everything has conspired to kill public enthusiasm for new commercial aircraft.

I consulted an old friend, Peter Flynn, who is the sales director for Airbus North America. He assured me that the A380 is an incredible airplane. It didn't sound like mere professional assurance. Peter was a U.S. Navy helicopter pilot during the Vietnam War and remembers when flying was a stimulating adventure, and then some.

Two months to the day after the A380 first became airborne Peter and I were at Airbus headquarters in Toulouse, France, in the A380 systems-testing facility. The outside of the building is as blank as a supertanker hull and about as big. Inside we stood on a glassed-fronted balcony three stories above the main floor looking at something called the "Iron Bird." This is a full-scale installation of all the mechanical, electrical, and hydraulic connections within an A380 and of all the moving parts to which they are joined except the engines. The Iron Bird was very busy trying out the levers, gears, cylinders, struts, and things-I-don't-know-the-names-of that work the landing gear, rudder, elevators, ailerons, and things-I-don't-know-the-names-of-either.

We think of a passenger plane as a pod, a capsule wafting through the atmosphere containing mainly us and, if we're lucky, our luggage. Jet power plants are simply automatic typhoons, effortlessly blowing hot air. And, while we fervently hope the jets continue to do that, it doesn't occur to us that an airliner has a greater confusion of innards than anything we dissected in science class, even if we went to med school.

I wonder what the ancient Romans would have divined from such entrails. Certainly not aviation. The Iron Bird couldn't have looked less avian. Nor—airplanes being made of aluminum and carbon fiber composites and such—was much ferrous metal involved. The iron in the Iron Bird was in the steel ramps and ladders branching over and through it so that engineers could go to and fro.

Our corporate tour guide, the cheerful and patient Debra Batson, manager for "scientific media," pointed out the Iron Bird's most important components. These looked to me like a tangle of extension cords from an overambitious attempt at outdoor Christmas lighting. Airbus was the first producer of commercial aircraft to make its planes all fly-by-wire. That is, there are no rods or cables—nothing that can be pushed or yanked—between the flier and the flown. Everything is accomplished by computer command. And I trust that the nosewheel pays more attention to its e-mail than I do to mine.

Debra pointed out the second most important components, which looked like a tangle of garden hoses from an attempt to put out the fire caused by the outdoor Christmas lighting. These were the hydraulic systems that operate the A380's control surfaces. In the A380 the pressure in the hydraulic system has been increased from the usual 3,000 pounds per square inch to 5,000 psi, making the system smaller, lighter, and as powerful as the kick to the back of my passenger seat from the child sitting behind me. The hydraulics also handle the braking on the A380's twenty-wheel main landing gear. "A New Dimension in Air Travel" informed me that "the brake is capable of stopping 45 double-decker buses traveling at 200 mph, simultaneously, in under 25 seconds." It is an ambition of mine to learn enough math to figure out comparisons like that and write them myself. But

I'm afraid I'd get carried away with digressions about what kind of engine you'd have to put in a double-decker bus to make it go that fast, where you'd drive it, how you'd find forty-four people to drive the other buses, and what would happen to the bus riders. At the moment, in the systems-testing facility, I was carried away with digressions about the miracle of engineering. It is not vouchsafed even to the Pope to see the very mechanism by which miracles are performed. Would the Pope be as confused by his kind of miracle as I was by the Iron Bird? Would this affect the doctrine of papal infallibility?

"Above my pay grade," Peter said. He and Debra and I went to the other side of the building to look at the cockpit simulators. These were arrayed along a wall and curtained off like private viewing booths for the kind of movie that isn't shown on airplanes. We peeked inside one booth. That kind of movie wasn't playing on the simulator's windscreen. A speeding runway came toward us, followed by dropping land, and enveloping haze, and more vertigo than we would have felt if the floor had moved. It hadn't. "Unfortunately," Peter said, "the rock-and-roll simulator was booked up today. You can crash that one. And it makes really embarrassing noises."

The simulator we were in was computer-linked to the Iron Bird. Two pilots in sport clothes sat at the controls while people with clipboards stood behind them taking notes. The pilots didn't seem to do much. Mostly they tapped on computer keyboards or fiddled with a trackball mouse. This was what was causing the frenetic activity in the Iron Bird—a teenager's immersion in Grand Theft Auto leading to an actual car's being stolen somewhere.

I sat in the pilot seat of another simulator. Peter took the copilot position. There wasn't even a jump seat for Debra.

"This whole big, damn thing," I said, "is flown by . . . you and me?"

"Yep," Peter said, "and it doesn't need me."

I, however, couldn't find any controls except rudder pedals to pump. I hope these weren't computer-linked to anything and that I didn't initiate wild yaw that knocked any Iron Bird engineers off their ramps and ladders. In front of me, instead of a yoke, was a foldout desktop. Perhaps these days the most important function of a pilot is to fill out Homeland Security forms with information on suspicious passengers.

"Look over to your left," Peter said.

"But it's like the joystick on an Atari game," I said.

"Yep," Peter said.

"Could you fly one of these?" I asked. "I mean, and land it?"

"Yep," Peter said. "The computers do all the work."

And there were a lot of computers—eight LCD screens. They showed . . . Well, they showed lots of things.

"I've never played Atari," I said.

Debra explained that the A380 has essentially the same computer hardware and, indeed, essentially the same cockpit as all Airbus aircraft, from the 107-seat A318 on up.

"So you just build a plane," I said, "and the cockpit plugs in like a memory stick."

"I don't think we put it that way in the promotional literature," Debra said.

The promotional literature cites the advantages of "Flight Operational Commonality." Airbus estimates that pilots of its A340 series aircraft, which carry 300 to 380 passengers, can be certified to fly the A380 with just a week or two of additional training, thanks to the adaptive flexibility of computer technology.

I've never been fond of computers the way I'm fond of the stuff that *I* call hardware. Computers seem a little too adaptively flexible, like the strange natives, odd societies, and head cases we study in the social sciences. There's more opposable thumb in the digital world than I care for; it's awfully close to human.

"Does spam ever pop up on the cockpit computer screens?" I asked. "Or random celebrity sex videos?"

"No," said Debra.

Debra took us to the A380 interior mock-up, to see how the humans that we'll be awfully close to will be seated on the A380. Toulouse, of course, is where Lautrec was from— he of perfect proportions for modern airline seating. But I didn't mention it. Debra did mention that Airbus has no final responsibility for what airlines do with the A380's interior, let alone for the behavior of the passengers. But Airbus tries to keep air steerage from being foisted on the public. And the designers of the A380 interior mock-up tried to wrest the graciously spacious from the ghastly vast.

Clever partitioning eliminated the tube-of-doom look and gave the rows of seats theater-like proportions. In theaters, after all, people regularly sit more tightly confined in harder chairs for worse ordeals than an airline flight. At least that was my experience with *Rent*. In the forward cabin wide steps rose to the upper deck, and in the tail a spiral staircase descended. For some reason a spiral staircase always adds zest to a setting. Perhaps it speaks to the DNA helix in us all.

Airbus wasn't trying to kid anyone with this mock-up. No bowling alleys, squash courts, or lap pools were to be seen. Instead there were a small duty-free shop, a couple of miniature barrooms where you could stand with your foot on the rail, a nook with built-in davenports, and other places in which you could stretch, be free and easy, and not feel you were trapped in a Broadway extravaganza and would catch hell from your wife and the eighteen people between you and the aisle if you bolted.

The first-class section, naturally, was supplied with those investment bankers' La-Z-Boys—Laissez-Faire-Boys, if you will—that can turn themselves into club chairs, chaise longues, or featherbeds and are equipped with buttons to press to get practically anything you want other than that celebrity in the sex video. Business class had something similar, with maybe one fewer caviar spoon and champagne bucket per customer.

But most of us travel as "gate freight." The A380's size is what seems to worry people, yet the size is also the selling point—offering potential comfort as well as potential low fares. The A380, although it contains 50 percent more room than a 747, is supposed to contain only 35 percent more seats. The A380's upper passenger deck is almost as wide as the main deck of a 747, and the lower one is 19 inches wider. Airbus says proudly—a little too proudly—that 1.3 inches in seat width is gained in economy class. This is modest progress. The 747 was introduced in 1970. I've gained 1.3 inches in seat width since the last time I bought pants.

Once you've girdled yourself into a seat, a better measure of comfort than width is what's termed pitch. This is the distance between my expanding posterior and the aching back of the person in front of me. Airbus wants seats to have a minimum pitch of 34 inches and urges airlines to choose the thinnest seat-back designs. But pitch space is lost to that Satan's looking glass, the in-seat video screen.

A 32-inch pitch, or even less, is common in the airline industry. I am five feet nine. Sitting in a living room chair I measure 26 inches from my wallet to the disappearance of my trouser creases. Add 4 inches for the TV-thickened seat in front of me, and stuff a 3-inch copy of the *Michelin Guide* into my seat-back pocket, and a 32-inch pitch means arthroscopic surgery.

In the economy section of the A380 mock-up, Airbus designers compensated for this dark truth with relentlessly cheerful carpet and upholstery in subtropical-fruit colors. I think they overdid it. One shade of citron pleaded to be called "Lemony Snicket." The mock-up also had a mood-lighting system that projected upon the cabin ceiling a beautiful morning, noon, or nighttime sky, according to the hour of the day. This would be perfectly unnecessary if the fool in the window seat would quit watching *Wedding Crashers*, open his shade, and look outside.

I looked outside myself, and a real A380 was standing on a taxiway. The Airbus corporate complex sprawls like an American Sunbelt development, but with the Toulouse airport at the center of it instead of a golf course. The A380 was a 3-wood and a 5-iron away. It didn't look so large. Then I noticed, next to the A380, a wide-body A340, the largest Airbus plane until now. The A340 was diminutive in its ordinary hugeness. Even so, the A380 was more impressive for its presence than for its bulk. The wingspan is 261 feet 8 inches—53 feet longer than an A340-600's. But there is a reassuring double amount of surface to the A380's wing. This wing is so thick where it meets the fuselage that you could park a car inside. The A380 cockpit, instead of being perched on the catbird seat like a 747's, is placed low in the fuselage, where the pilots can mind their business with the ground. It gave the plane a high-foreheaded, thoughtful look.

The A380 in fact has not two but three decks—the lowest devoted to luggage, freight, and crew rest facilities for long-range flights. The decks are contained in an oval cross section with a smooth, sailing ship curve. The wings sweep back at thirty-three degrees, almost into the shape of a jib, and the stabilizer fin is as wide and tall and rakishly set as a Cunard funnel. The A380 seemed nautical—more liner than airliner. No one ever quailed at the prospect of the *Queen Mary 2*'s carrying 720 passengers.

"Five hundred and fifty-five," Debra corrected.

The A380—the only one flying at that time—taxied away, then turned and rolled in our direction. Now it did look like an airplane, carrying itself with dignity and tending a bit to embonpoint. It had none of the fashionable emaciation of the old 707, with its gaunt runway-model (as it were) looks. Nor did it have the DC-10's scary put-the-engines-anywhere accessorizing style. Rather, the A380 had *ton.* (And tonnage.)

"Can I get on a test ride?" I asked.

"No," Debra said.

"Why?"

"Insurance," Peter said.

Insurance is not usually a romantic word, but think of death and all the other romantic things there are to be insured against. Maybe aviation hasn't lost its glamour. The A380 rose decisively, and before I thought it would. A 747 needs a third of a mile more to take off. The A380 flew over our heads with a Brobdingnagian whisper. It makes half a 747's noise. And then the A380 flew away, into a haze very similar to the haze projected on the windshield of the A380 cockpit simulator. Let the haze stand for predictions about the future of travel. Will it ever be fun again?

Anyway, building an A380 seemed like fun. Debra and Peter and I went to the production line. Surprise at the scale of the A380 was quieted by surprise at the scale of the place where three more of them were being built. I did not know there was so much indoors. The factory, Debra said, can be seen from space.

Actually, the A380 is built all over Europe. This was the final-assembly plant. The plane arrives in seven pieces sounding like some provincial soup recipe: three slices of fuselage, two wings, a fin, and a tail. The parts come to Toulouse by way of ocean freighters, canal barges, road convoys, and Airbus's whale-shaped and more than whale-sized Beluga transport plane. (Measured by cargo volume, the Beluga is even larger than the A380.) I particularly liked picturing whole wings and great cabin sections strapped to humble barges, bringing a bit of industrial reality (and swamped decks) to people taking those French canal-boat tours and trying to pretend that travel is fun.

The constituent parts of an A380 are placed in a single enormous jig—a Jell-O mold with the miniature marshmallows, fruit slices, and nutmeats aligned by means of laser technology to degrees of precision that take a lot of zeros behind a variety of decimal points to express.

Engineering miracles have always required genius, but the miraculousness has gotten to a point where comparable genius is needed to explain it. Fortunately, a genius showed us around the factory. This was Charles Champion, an Airbus executive vice president and the head of the A380 program since the project was launched, nearly five years before. Champion has since been promoted to chief operating officer of Airbus. (And, after this was written, demoted again, for slowness in bringing the A380 to fruition.) But he is, first, an engineer. And he all but glowed with enjoyment of the A380's engineering. For example, the A380's wings are clad in an esoteric alloy, what an ordinary mechanical engineer would call "unobtainium." The wing panels are up to 180 feet long and 9 feet wide, and in places they are only $1/_8$ inch thick. They need to hold a "double curved aerodynamic shape." The way to achieve this is with a twenty-four-hour application of varying temperatures and loads to create "stress relaxation" and "permanent deformation." The process is called "creep age forming" and, opportunities for Michael Jackson wisecracks aside, I have no idea what I'm talking about.

But Charles Champion did. And he made everything, if not exactly clear, clearly exciting.

Peter was looking around as if he were on a machinery Mount Olympus, watching the powers of the firmament come together, this Leda mating with (aided by laser technology) that swan. Peter is a romantic about machines. When he was a helicopter pilot, machines saved his life any number of times. Of course it was machines that put his life in jeopardy. But that's romance.

Charles Champion told us how the first A380 built wasn't flown but was towed to a static test platform, where its wings and fuselage were twisted and bent and loaded with weights until the plane was destroyed.

"That must have been horrible," I said "to see that happen to your first A380."

"Engineers love to break things," Champion said.

And French industrial workers love to make them. At

least they seemed to at Airbus. The assembly plant had a calm, cheerful, collegial air. Everything was tidy and well lit. Only the most muffled noises of manufacture could be heard. If Charles Dickens had visited Airbus he might have given up on the frenzied life of writing and lecturing that eventually killed him and reconsidered the blacking factory.

It had been a day of reconsideration for me, too. I was reconsidering my free-trade principles. The governments of France, Germany, Britain, and other European Union countries have "invested" in the A380. Boeing calls this a subsidy and has gone off in a snit to the World Trade Organization—as if Boeing didn't sell *Air Force One* to the U.S. government for a pretty penny. Should I be upset that taxes on Europeans will help pay for American airfares?

I was reconsidering my free-market ideals, as well. Charles Champion said that among the difficulties of the A380 program were the political considerations of which factories were to make what where. The result, it seems to me, is that the most expensive parts, such as the wings and cockpit, are manufactured in the most expensive places, such as England and France. A Chinese electronics company might as well outsource production to Manhattan. But do we really want Guatemalan child laborers sewing the treads to the tires on our landing gear?

And I was reconsidering the French. They were welcoming at Airbus and everywhere else in Toulouse. They didn't make fun of Peter when he spoke their language or me when I spoke mine. Food was *magnifique*. Manners were *charmant*.

At a *magnifique* lunch given in the Airbus executive dining room by the elegant Barbara Kracht, the vice president of media relations, manners had remained *charmant* even when I'd asked her, "What's with the *bus*?"

"You could have called the company," I'd said, "'Air-phaeton,' 'Airlimousine,' even 'Airyacht.'" She had responded politely, saying that when Airbus was founded, in 1970, it was still difficult to get people to think of flying as an ordinary means of transportation. We've gotten over that little hurdle.

One thing I wasn't reconsidering was air travel. I had a flight home the next day and was trying not to think about it—with some success, considering that I was standing next to a device to provide the most air travel in history. We were on a platform beside a nearly completed A380. The wingtip was just above our heads. "Go ahead," Charles Champion said to me. "Grab it." I reached up and tentatively curled my fingers over the metal. "Now pull down," he said.

The A380 wing is one of the mightiest structures ever created—9,100 square feet of ribs, spars, and skin able to thrust itself out 147 feet into nothingness and give lift to its half of 1,235,000 pounds. I pulled, and this great formation bowed to my eye level, supple as a living thing.

With the whole wing flexing at my light grasp, all the poetic, fanciful wonder of living in the twenty-first century came back to me. I'd outdone Keats and Shelley in matters of the sublime. It touched them. I touched it.

I was full of quixotic fervor. I would fly on an A380 straight to hell. And, unless airport amenities, immigration clearance, baggage delivery, customs inspection, and the courtesy of security personnel improve dramatically before the A380 goes into service, I will.

7

IF YOU THINK MODERN LIFE IS AWFUL, YOU HAVEN'T SEEN MODERN ART

Venice Biennale, July 2005

❖

How bad does modern art stink? Every two years since 1895 (war and such allowing) the Venice Biennale has gathered new masterpieces from around the world in a place and at a season where the reek of genius can be accurately compared to the warm-weather aroma of the Grand Canal. Dr. Johnson defined art as "the power of doing something which is not taught by nature." What's in the canal is something nature teaches us to do from our first hours of infancy. It is as nothing to the power of art.

Like most sensible people, you probably lost interest in modern art about the time that Julian Schnabel was painting broken pieces of the crockery that his wife had thrown at him for painting broken pieces of crockery instead of painting the bathroom and hall. Or maybe you lost interest back when Andy Warhol silk-screened canned lunch for the kiddies and oddments from under the kitchen sink. There's been so much to be so uninterested in. And yet, astonishingly, modern art has gotten less interesting. I didn't know this. I was more prepared to be irked than bored. The Biennale consists of national pavilions, mostly from Europe or Europe-aping countries. One or more brilliant creative types are selected to fly the flag. Given how Europeans feel about America, I doubted many of the flags flown would be the Stars and Stripes. There are also two curated shows, the largest in the Arsenale, the former Pentagon of Venice. The city-state projected its great military and commercial might from the Arsenale, which now sits empty between art shows, nicely symbolizing progress of the arts, other than the arty ones, in Europe today: arts of manufacture, diplomacy, and war.

But I wander from the irksome subject at hand. The curators of the shows are, for the first time in fifty-one Biennales, women. Thus I expected to be hectored or, I should say, Hecubaed. Rosa Martinez and Maria de Corral are also from Spain, a nation that reacted to terrorism by promptly reverting to socialism at home and poltroonery abroad. Aren't those the preferred artistic policies? I assumed modern artists were all members of the great bohemian turkey flock of ardent individualists, looking up with beaks uniformly agape at identical high ideals of world peace, economic justice, ecological harmony, and government funding for the arts. Before my visit to the Biennale I supposed that all artists thought alike. It never occurred to me that they didn't think at all. For example, German artist Gregor Schneider wanted to reproduce the Ka'bah of Mecca full scale in the

Piazza San Marco. Imagine the delight of Islamic fundamentalists at slews of American cruise ship day trippers and half a million pigeons on *hajj*. Authorities in Venice demurred, and Schneider was reduced to playing with PhotoShop on his Macintosh. (Although computer-generated artificial intelligence eludes us, artificial stupidity has been perfected.)

But most of the Biennale's thoughtlessness did not produce thoughts of potential consequences or (I've checked my notes) any thoughts at all. Mona Hatoum from Lebanon built a ten-foot-wide circular sandbox with a pair of motorized blades mounted in the center. One blade raked ridges in the sand while the other smoothed them out—an automatic Zen garden, the lazy way to a perfectly empty mind. And Italy's Bruna Esposito scattered onion skins on marble floor tiles and, remarkably, did not title it *Get the Broom*.

Dimbulb was more than a metaphor at the Biennale. It was often too dark in the galleries to read the names of the works and artists. As if I cared. Somebody put a bunch of portable typewriters missing most of their keys on school desks so that the thoughts of art lovers could be thumbtacked to the wall. I quote one verbatim: "......8888889999993333." Someone else tied a blindfolded teddy bear to a stick in a roomful of upholstery with the stuffing yanked out. It's not your-kid-can-do-this art. Your kid does this and you're on the phone to the child psychiatrist. Didacticism was to be found, of course. Argentinean Sergio Vega urged Biennale patrons to have their photograph taken next to a hand-cuffed mannequin with a burlap bag over its head. Alas for poor PFC Lynndie England, of Abu Ghraib snapshot fame, if only she'd been an aesthetic type. And the first thing I saw on entering the Arsenale was manifestos from some U.S. art collective calling itself Guerrilla Girls. Among these was a parody of a movie poster: *The Birth of Feminism* starring Pamela Anderson as Gloria Steinem, Halle Berry as Flo Kennedy, etc. The tagline: "They made women's rights look good. Really good." As the devil whispered to Rudyard Kipling (but recused himself from whispering to the Guerrilla Girls), "It's clever, but is it art?"

Actually it's not clever. The Guerrilla Girls are too young to remember what a babe Gloria Steinem was. She made Pamela Anderson look like, well, Flo Kennedy. And the Guerrilla Girls are too old to realize how beside the point their point is.

Here's Indy driver Danica Patrick interviewed in *Newsweek*:

"Are you the Gloria Steinem of racing?"

"The what? I don't even know who that is."

Hanging beside the blather was a chandelier fashioned by Joana Vasconcelos from 14,000 tampons. Maybe this was an indignant statement about drudgery enforced by gender constructs—darn hard to light for dinner parties. Maybe this was an ironic commentary on a visit to Venice where everybody's wife wants to buy a great big incredibly expensive Murano glass chandelier. Or maybe this was just a waste of time. The modern art of 2005 wastes more time than the modern art of yore did. You could walk right by a Jackson Pollock drip canvas in half a second. Not so with the dominant creative medium of the Biennale, video art, the finger paint of the twenty-first century. I experienced, as quickly as I could, thirty-six examples of the form and doubtless missed many others because I would stumble into pitch-black exhibition spaces that smelled strongly of face-pierced video art aficionados and would bolt before anything video happened. Also, there were a number of national pavilions, such as Albania's, that I wasn't able to find.

Herewith a sampling of Boring Video Downloads, or BVDs: lonely-looking people talking to the camera; lonely-looking people not talking to the camera; people looking lonely; people with lightbulbs over their heads, which would indicate ideas if this were a comic strip but since this is video art it doesn't; the Rosetta stone being dusted; pictures of an empty movie theater; pictures from an empty movie projector; someone's sweaty, hairy back; a city skyline with trash piling up in the foreground in the shape of the skyscrapers (get it?); a fellow who has turned a kitchen table upside down, attached an outboard motor to it, and is cruising across a bay; a man in a bear suit living in the Berlin zoo; cardboard cartons rigged with overhead projectors so that viewers look into boxes full of little naked people engaged in mildly prurient activities; a man in a waterfall with real water falling in front of the video screen (get it?); and an imaginary trailer for an imaginary remake of Bob Guccione's all-too-real 1979 smut-flop *Caligula* featuring—in a successful attempt to capture the alpha of boring and the omega of thoughtlessness—guest appearances by Gore Vidal and Courtney Love. John Stuart Mill said that the purpose of art is "the employment of the powers of nature for an end." Specifically, the huge, flabby hind end of a transvestite named Leigh Bowery in a video showing spring-loaded clothespins being attached to tender parts of his body. He deserved it. Nearby was Regina José Galindo's video of herself having her hymen surgically restored in extreme close-up. I will forgo description of the luncheon fare available at the Biennale. Fabulous Italian food may be of interest to readers, but not on the way back up. (Memo to video auteurs: There already is a method of turning moving pictures into art. It's been in use since *The Birth of a Nation*.)

Among the many uninteresting things about the Biennale was the dearth of artworks that you'd like to have or to hold or to look at again as long as you live even if they were done by a beloved (if psychiatrically disturbed) son or daughter. The aptly named Louise Bourgeois had some aluminum sculptures that were blobby and intestinal in a nice kind of way and would look great on my mantel if my mantel were three feet wide. And I was enthralled by Subhoda Gupta's rows and rows of stainless steel shelving carefully stacked with pristine cooking utensils. Gupta, who is Indian, went straight to the point with his title: *Curry*. My guess is that he's not an artist at all but is bucking for a green card as a kitchen designer.

In the entire Biennale there was exactly one good new artist, Ricky Swallow, lone exhibitor at the unprepossessing, not to say prefab, Australian pavilion. Swallow created a full-size tableau of a seafood catch spread ready for the cook with the tablecloth pushed to one side of the table and including lobster, mullet, a bucket of oysters, and a half-peeled lemon all seemingly carved from a single block of maple. Among Swallow's other brilliant whittlings was a medallion of hanging game in the manner of the eighteenth-century master British woodworker Grinling Gibbons, but with a couple of wild-card Aussie lizards thrown in. And there was a perfectly rendered bike helmet with serpents entwined among the straps and ventilation slots. That's my opinion of the Tour de France, too. The docent at the pavilion, instead of busily looking aloof like his counterparts, said "G'day, mate."

The Czech pavilion had a lot of ball bearings on the floor. In the German pavilion people had been hired to yell at you. The Icelandic pavilion was made from twigs and branches.

Icelanders respect nature so much they've given their beavers MFAs. The Hungarian pavilion was full of deep-sea-diving suits dressed in pajamas and wellie boots. The Swiss pavilion had an enormous digital clock ticking off the "5 Billion Year Countdown Until the Explosion of the Sun." Cuckoo. The Austrian pavilion was entirely built over in a shapeless jumble that looked like someone had taken Frank Gehry's titanium away and made him work in two-by-fours and tar paper. It was an improvement on Gehry Partners' Walt Disney Concert Hall in Los Angeles.

The U.S. pavilion featured talentless airbrush artist Ed Ruscha's airbrush renderings of industrial buildings of no note. But the air-conditioning was excellent. An Argentinean artist built a room from Sheetrock and punched a lot of holes through the walls. Who can blame him? The air-conditioning wasn't functioning at all in there. I saw an impressive constructivist work of bolted steel and wire mesh, but it turned out to be the Arsenale's freight elevator. Phone kiosks in the shape of giant fiberglass parrots with receivers and dial pads between their wings seemed better than art until I discovered they *were* art. Title: *Global Warming*. Jennifer Allora and Guillermo Calzadilla created a beautiful hippopotamus in heroic scale, but they sculpted it from that noble material, that enduring element, mud. Crumpled newspaper was scattered around, I guess so you could wipe the hippo off your feet before going on to the next exhibit. Pascale Marthine Tayou tangled hundreds of plastic shopping bags into a net to create a scene identical to roadside fences all over the third world. In fairness, Tayou is from Cameroon. And the sophomoric smart-ass mouth-breathing medal goes to Daniel Knorr of Romania, who left the Romanian pavilion empty and called it *European Influenza*.

Still, I departed the Venice Biennale with joy in my heart—partly because I was glad to leave, but more so from learning that all the awful people whose oeuvres I had just endured have something to keep them busy. In another era such crackpots would have been excluded by sheer lack of skill and knowledge from any involvement with the fine arts, the way Hitler was. He retreated to grubby beer halls, compensating for his thwarted ambitions by concocting insane demagoguery. It wouldn't happen today. Hitler's complete artistic incompetence would find a welcome home at the Biennale.

It could be that all awful dictators are frustrated artists—Mao with his poetry and Mussolini with his monuments. Stalin was once a journalistic hack, and I can personally testify to how frustrated they are. Pol Pot left a very edgy photo collection behind. And Osama seems quite interested in video.

Stupid art saps stupid ideology. You could see it in the Chinese pavilion. One installation was a scrap metal and tinfoil contraption that a Chinese farmer built believing it could fly him to the moon. The farmer was included in the installation. Then there was a BVD of a crowded city street. Every now and then somebody the crowd couldn't see shouted loudly. Members of the crowd would look around as though a crazy person was loose, then go about their business. And China's supposedly most talented young architect, Yung Ho Chang, made a big, long tangle of bamboo poles. This was in no way as impressive, or for that matter as intimidating, as the bamboo scaffolding surrounding each construction site for the topless towers of Shanghai. If national pavilions are anything to go by, the fearsome Communist juggernaut of Asia is headed toward being an Iceland of ideological power.

And what of the *demos* who fall for demagoguery? Venice is certainly full of these this time of year. Hosts and swarms of them come in a state of idiocy evident in their dress and bodily form—so much so that a certain well-known span to the ducal palace should be renamed the Bridge of Thighs. But the masses were giving the Biennale a good leaving-alone. The few visitors to the pavilions and exhibition halls were people who looked like they make what it looked like they liked, or will make some when the drugs wear off. It is a hopeful sign for worldwide democracy that even the dull, vapid summer tourists of Venice are too smart for art.

8

My Wife's Got a Gun

Brays Island Plantation, South Carolina, February 2006

❖

Mrs. O. is afraid of birds—not terrified, not "chicken," as it were, and not exactly phobic. She just considers birds to be air lizards, icky velociraptors in bad boas. The Galápagos trip with George and Laura would have been a misery for her. When we were looking at the Lindblad Expeditions brochure, Mrs. O.'s reaction was, "The blue-footed boobies waddle *right up to you?* Ugh!" I'm not saying she got pregnant with our youngest child, Buster, just to avoid the Galápagos cruise, but . . .

I, on the other hand, love birds. I spend a lot of money every year and travel thousands of miles for my love of birds. I trudge across acres of muddy fields, push through tangles of forest underbrush, and hunker in swamps at dawn simply to find birds—and kill them. Call it tough love.

Every good marriage is a compromise. For years, Mrs. O. displayed no nervous symptoms about mallards in the freezer, as long as the gutting and plucking had been done somewhere other than her kitchen (or laundry room, as I had occasion to be reminded). And I didn't go after pheasants in South Dakota on our wedding anniversary. Then one day Mrs. O. said, "I want to learn to shoot. I want to go bird hunting." Why? A more recently married person would have asked that aloud. But if I suddenly said, "I want to learn to empty the dishwasher. I want to get up in the middle of the night when the kids cry," Mrs. O. wouldn't check the medicine chest to see what I'd been taking until later. She'd say, "Great!"

I said, "Great!" But I was worried. Mrs. O. wanted to learn to shoot. I mentally reviewed my recent behavior. I was pretty sure she was using "shoot" as an intransitive verb. I didn't think I detected an elision of "you" at the end of the sentence. Maybe Mrs. O. had been listening to me. It's always worrisome when a spouse does that. I'd been telling her that the way to get over her fear of birds was to go hunting. "Shoot at them," I advised, "and after you miss the little SOB's three or four times in a row, you won't be scared, you'll be angry." Did I really want an angry wife?

Or maybe something had happened on a recent trip to London, when I'd dragged Mrs. O. to the Holland & Holland store. While I'd been drooling over shotguns, perhaps she'd realized that the field sports present a whole new head-to-toe wardrobe opportunity. A flash of pain ran through my Visa card.

Also, I was concerned that if Mrs. O. tried bird hunting, she'd end up hating it. I privately suspect that men and women are different. They don't always enjoy the same things or enjoy them in the same ways. No doubt, when our children came along, Mrs. O. had similar anxieties about gender-based tastes and inclinations. Probably she was secretly relieved and surprised that I didn't eat the kids. I thought I'd have to make bird hunting somehow posh, festive, and feminine. How would she, I asked myself, go about convincing me that changing diapers and singing lullabies at four a.m. is as much of a good time as sitting shivering and soaked in a duck blind at about the same time of day?

Actually, with proper application of Jack Daniel's, either can be fun. But women, in my experience, are not quite so easily convinced that they are enjoying themselves. I called my friends Perry and Sally Harvey and wangled an invitation to Brays Island, a swell quail plantation in South Carolina.

Brays Island is 5,500 acres of tidewater landscape on the Pocotaligo River not far from Hilton Head. It's pretty much how I picture heaven, with, in the first place, a membership too exclusive to include me. The vast woods and fields and the miles of waterways and marshes are full of wildlife. Besides the quail there's shooting for Hungarian partridge, chukar, pheasants, doves, ducks, turkey, and deer. Largemouth bass lurk in the freshwater ponds. The Pocotaligo is replete with redfish, black drum, and flounder. In the nearby blue water are sea trout, stripers, bluefish, and tarpon. If these pleasures should pall there are skeet, trap, sporting clays, an eighteen-hole private golf course, tennis, a pool, a twenty-five-stall boarding stable, and forty miles of equestrian trails. The weather is admittedly less like paradise and more like the opposite during the summer, and Brays probably has more gunfire and dead animals than heaven does. Maybe it's the heaven that dogs go to, which, truthfully, is the one I'd prefer. The plantation has forty bird dogs, in kennels larger and cleaner than my old bachelor apartment ever was. I suppose Brays isn't heaven for quail and redfish, although, on my previous visits, these critters seemed immortal enough when I would blast or cast.

I usually hunt in places that are, frankly, more purgatorial. But I figured that Mrs. O. has years to learn about bird season accommodations of the "Fur Seasons" and "Itch-Carlton" kind. No need to introduce her immediately to the toilet facilities of an Arkansas duck shack. She doesn't have to know, yet, that the most productive woodcock cover in New Hampshire is an old town dump.

The entrance to Brays is a mile-long avenue of white board fences without a paint flake or knothole stain in sight. The meadows are so well-tended that only the presence of real stable grooms instead of the cast-iron kind distinguishes the fields from suburban lawns. Ancient live oaks rise, arboreal castles with green baileys, green keeps, green crenellations, and—to strain a metaphor—heraldic banners of Spanish moss. This doesn't look like a place to shoot birds. This looks like a place to marry off Scarlett O'Hara, except without the liberal guilt. General Sherman's troops, on their flamboyant (in the root sense of the word) march to the sea, burned the original Brays Plantation Manor and distributed some of the plantation land to emancipated slaves. Instead of a ticky-tacky Tara of doubtful provenance, the main house at Brays is a handsome white-brick Federalist-revival spread built with modern plumbing and laborsaving kitchen appliances in the 1930s by Francis B. Davis Jr. of the firmly Yankee United States Rubber Company. The Davis home has been converted to guest quarters, dining rooms, and a bar for the Brays Island members. And (heaven again) the food is worth dying for. Only one thing was wrong with Brays Island on our first morning there—pouring rain.

"Darn," said Mrs. O. "We'll have to go shopping."

"Fortunately," I said, "I brought an extra pair of rain pants. Put a hand towel inside your Barbour coat collar so the water doesn't run down the back of your neck. We'll have to kick the birds up a bit. They won't be flying very well in this weather. Don't shoot at them if they just hop; you don't want to hit the dogs. And don't worry about rattlesnakes when we're stomping around in the brush; when it's chilly and wet like this they're not very active. Let's get going."

"Why?" said Mrs. O.

And I have to admit, she had me there. I thought about all the time I've spent hunting upland birds in inclement weather, usually getting skunked. "So we can be wet and uncomfortable," I said. "And not have very good shooting and probably catch cold."

"Are you crazy?" said Mrs. O.

We went shopping. The nearby town of Beaufort, South Carolina, is very cute and quaint. It has a large, large number of antique stores. As near as I can tell, shopping is, for women, what hunting is for men. Except that they never get to use the remote control, battery-operated electric-shock dog collar on misbehaving store owners who are supposed to be helping them hunt for antiques. Also, as far as I'm concerned, a lot of antiques look like somebody's shot them already.

Then we toured Brays with Sally and Perry Harvey. The former cattle ranch was sold to the Pingree family in the 1960s. They turned it into a development centered on hunting and fishing. The land-use concept was based on an idea of Frank Lloyd Wright's. Each of the 325 house sites is a one-acre circle surrounded by common land. The sites are screened from one another. Membership in Brays Island is limited to lot owners, and the members own the plantation.

A few sites were still for sale. One looked out over the river toward a bald eagle sanctuary in the distance. I could see Mrs. O. eyeing the spot with a hunter's—a house hunter's—rapt gaze. Imaginary swing sets and fictive bikes and Zip scooters were beginning to materialize in the rain.

"I came down here from Aspen to visit a friend," Perry told me. "And I fell in love with the place. I was out all day, fishing in the morning and shooting quail in the afternoon. When I got back that night, Sally had bought a lot."

"Sally and I are going over to look at the new tennis courts," said Mrs. O.

"And I'm sticking right with you," I said.

The rain stopped about four, and Mrs. O. took a shooting lesson from the manager of the Brays shooting club, Greg Freeman. I stepped aside on the theory that spouses should never get pedagogical with each other. We've been through this at home with Mrs. O. trying to teach me to unload the dishwasher. Greg went through the rudiments of gun safety and put Mrs. O. on the No. 4 pad on the skeet field. He launched a clay pigeon from the high house. She missed. Greg stepped forward and spoke to Mrs. O. briefly. He launched another speedy pass shot from the high house. She broke it. And the next one. And the next.

After forty years of shooting I get a hit on No. 4 high house about as often as Ozzy Osbourne gets one on the *Billboard* Top 40.

"I've noticed this before," I said to Greg. "Women are good at learning to use a shotgun. Even if they've never shot before, it only takes a little bit of instruction. Why is that?"

"Women listen," said Greg.

And I try to listen too, except after forty years of shooting I don't hear very well—as I've explained more than once when I didn't get up in the middle of the night when the kids were crying. "You hear the little 'ping' from the microwave OK," said Mrs. O., "if burritos are defrosting."

When Mrs. O. had rendered the clay pigeon a pretty much extinct species I asked her, "What did Greg tell you?"

"He told me to put my weight forward and quit thinking about it. He said, 'Lower your IQ to fifty.'" No wonder men don't listen. My IQ has been down there since puberty, and if I put any more weight forward I'm going to have to give up on Brooks Brothers and get that artist, Christo, who draped the Pont Neuf in bedsheets, to wrap my gut as an art project.

The next morning was cool and bright. Brays Island has a picturesque mule wagon that carried Perry, Sally, Mrs. O., and me into the quail fields. The guides and the dogs followed, less picturesquely, in pickup trucks. We could have ridden horses to the covers, if we'd wanted to be over-the-top picturesque.

Most quail shot east of the Mississippi are raised in pens and set out for the benefit of sportsmen. Thus, as shopping is hunting for women, hunting is shopping for men—a visit to the poultry department at Safeway, although Perdue roasters never have a chance to fly away unscathed and make me look like a fool.

The hunting grounds at Brays are laid out in the old cattle pastures and among the groves of live oaks. The fields are carefully sown with the right vegetation and selectively brush-hogged. The men in charge of the quail pens make sure that the birds are acclimatized—so they'll covey up the way they do in nature and fly well when flushed. Land

that's been settled since the 1600s requires a lot of cultivation to make it wild. Senior guide Billy Aiken has a good ol'
boy's accent. However, it's in Latin. He knows the taxonomic
name of every plant in the quail fields. He has degrees in
these things.

"So," said Mrs. O., "there's basically no point to hunting.
Everybody just goes to a lot of bother to shoot little quail."

"Um, yes," I said.

Mrs. O. eyed the grass tangles where the birds, which
discomfort her so, were hiding. "I can understand that,"
she said.

Billy and fellow guide Bryan opened their kennels, re-
leasing seventy-some pounds of English pointers, Boomer
and Pal.

"Good doggies!" said Mrs. O., whose loathing of birds
is matched by such affection for dogs that she cried at the
end of *Cujo* because the rabid Saint Bernard died.

"These aren't pets," I warned her. "These are serious
working dogs." The serious working dogs trotted over to
Mrs. O., licked her face, and rolled on their backs to have
their tummies scratched.

Mrs. O. and Perry lined up at a cover with Billy in the
middle and Boomer quartering all over the place. Boomer
pointed an Audubon Society calendar photograph of a
covey—a perfect feathered rondel of quail backed against
each other and ready to fly in every direction. Billy had
Mrs. O. walk in. I held my breath. A big quail flush is a
myocardial rupture moment for even the hardened nimrod.
There was a great burst of birds at Mrs. O.'s feet; a convulsion
of quail rose in her face. This must have been a nightmare
for her, an Imax screening of Hitchcock's *The Birds* with her
eyelids taped open. I mean this is the woman who calls me

at work when there are pigeons on the kitchen windowsill. Mrs. O. didn't flinch.

"It would have embarrassed Boomer," she said.

Mrs. O. didn't flinch, but on the other hand, Mrs. O. didn't shoot, either. "I was afraid I'd hit that tree," she explained to Billy.

He was a model of tact, explaining the harmlessness of No. 7 shot to a mature live oak. Boomer pointed more birds. This time Mrs. O. did shoot, but she shot from the hip. "Because my shoulder hurts from yesterday's shooting lesson," she stated with precise feminine logic.

Billy, who probably should be our nation's ambassador to the UN, where ability to suppress laughter is a vital asset, said, "Next time think one-two-three-four. Lift the gun to your shoulder, press your cheek to the stock, push the safety forward, pull the trigger back. One-two-three-four. Lift, press, push, pull."

Mrs. O., being a woman, listened. Boomer flushed a madhouse covey, bigger than the first and flying harder. Mrs. O. turned her gun on a particular bird. There was a puff of feathers, and a perpendicular drop. Boomer brought the quail to her feet.

Billy picked up the bird and Mrs. O. backed away. Billy thought she was having a PETA moment of animal cruelty regret. "Aw," he said, "it's not like it would have lived very long in the wild."

"Why don't you let Boomer make sure it's completely dead?" said Mrs. O.

That night we had dinner with Sally and Perry. "Well," said Sally, "how do you like birds now?"

"With quince preserves and curried rice, thank you," said Mrs. O., spearing another air lizard on the serving fork.

9

A Freedom Ride through China
Spring 2006

❖

Isn't China supposed to be moving toward political liberty? I believe the theory is that as an autocratic nation grows more prosperous, a middle class with socioeconomic influence arises. This middle class then exerts its influence on government by convening a Long Parliament, beheading King Charles, having an American Revolution, rolling tumbrels full of aristocrats through the streets of Paris, storming a Winter Palace, and things like that. The result is freedom and democracy for all, albeit with certain delays while the less estimable members of the middle class such as Cromwell, Napoleon, Lenin, Mussolini, Stalin, Hitler, and Mao get sorted.

And so it seemed to be going in China, back in 1989 in Tiananmen Square. But then China's political development took a left turn, or a right turn (depending on your framework of political analysis)—a wrong turn, anyway.

Freedom House is a private, nonprofit, bipartisan organization that promotes international freedom and democracy. It was founded in 1941 by Eleanor Roosevelt and Wendell Willkie, the man who'd lost the 1940 presidential election to Eleanor's husband. Eleanor and Wendell (odd bedfellows though they may have been—though not literally) were concerned by totalitarianism's growing threats to peace and liberty. Freedom House remains concerned. Me too, especially about China.

China represents a large percentage of the world's population and an ever-larger percentage of the world's production of material goods. That's a big chunk of unfreedom and nondemocracy. One of the main wheels on the planet's vehicle of liberty is seized up.

Besides promoting freedom and democracy, Freedom House also monitors them. Each year Freedom House publishes *Freedom in the World*, a thick, scholarly tome surveying political rights and civil liberties in every nation and territory. Scores are given for Political Rights and Civil Liberties on a scale of 1 to 7, 1 being as politically righteous or as civilly liberated as human nature allows and 7 being completely otherwise. China, in the years since the events in Tiananmen Square, has gone from a score of 7 for Political Rights and 6 for Civil Liberties to a score of 7 for Political Rights and 6 for Civil Liberties. Freedom House gives nations and territories one of three overall ratings: "Free," "Partly Free," and "Not Free." China is rated "Not Free." By measurable standards, freedom in China has changed very little since Freedom House initiated its scores and ratings half a century ago.

Yet Freedom House, although I respect its research and objectivity and served for years on its board, cannot be exactly right. The mere increase in China's prosperity must mean that more Chinese have greater wherewithal to exercise some aspects of free will. Certainly the Chinese are more free now than they were during the Great Leap Forward, when millions lost all their freedoms by starving to death. And the Chinese are more free to go about their business than they were during the Cultural Revolution, when there was no business to go about.

Measurement of freedom is difficult. A fairly accurate calculation can be made of the degree to which people can speak their minds, practice their religions, organize labor unions, or gather for political protests. People either do or don't have rights to vote, receive fair trials, and be secure in their homes and their personal lives. How well those rights are honored can be gauged. But once people rise above a subsistence level of economics (a subject about which Freedom House pretends no expertise), and material freedoms come into play, there are suddenly 1.3 billion different wants and needs. Humans are notoriously bad at figuring out what these are, even for themselves. And we are neither very accurate nor very generous when we estimate the wants and needs of others or their freedom to obtain them.

Freedom and democracy are abstract. Quotidian existence is conducted mostly in the world of things and stuff.

I went to China to take a tour of the world of things and stuff. I traveled with old friends, whom I'll call Tom and Mai. Tom is a Californian who's lived in Hong Kong for decades, working in the mining and metallurgy business. He was breaking ground on a pelletized iron ore processing plant in Nanjing. Tom seems to know everyone in China who has anything to do with iron, steel, coal, or drinking beer. Tom's wife, Mai, and her brothers, Hong Kong natives, had owned, until recently, a company that brokered textile machinery. When China began its "open-door" economic policy, Mai had the job of taking mainland clients to Europe (where they'd encounter their first fork, escalator, lingerie shop, etc.) and arranging for them to purchase used spinning, weaving, and dyeing equipment.

Everywhere Tom, Mai, and I went we were involved in the facts of China, not the ideas of China. Although Tom's and Mai's friends and business associates shared one idea—to banquet the three of us to death. At one meal in Chongqing there was a communal pot of boiling oil laced with chilies that could be used to commit arson. Raw ingredients were heaped upon our plates, and, using our chopsticks fondue-style, we cooked—I kept a list—two kinds of tripe, quail eggs, eels, chicken stomachs, chicken intestines, some very scary-looking fish, and the kind of sprouts that were about to turn into the beanstalk that Jack climbed.

Mai is fluent in English, Cantonese, and Mandarin. With her help I talked to people who worked in private enterprise and people who worked in government and people who worked on furthering cooperation between the two. That is, I talked to the kind of people who are necessary to the advocacy of freedom and democracy but who, so far, don't seem to be advocating it. They were forthcoming enough about their government, but they didn't care—or didn't care to say—much about the political theory of it. In Tom's opinion, "Their attitude is, 'Shhh . . . Politics is sleeping; don't wake it up.'" I wanted to know what the Chinese think about politics when politics is not what they're thinking about. Maybe we should be listening to what they don't say.

I was in Shanghai in 1997, and it looked like a knockoff of a great city, a sort of made-in-Hong-Kong Hong Kong. Everything had been built yesterday. And they'd built a lot of it—more than they seemed to have any use for. There was a marsh called Pudong on the far side of the Huangpu River where the ground was so low-lying that the water and sewer pipes had to be suspended above the pavement. Pudong was dotted with empty office complexes and buildings full of unrented apartments.

Now Pudong is some of the most expensive real estate on earth. Mai, Tom, and I stopped at a condominium where the sale price was $10,000 per square meter. Despite arriving in a chauffeured car wearing our corporate boardroom clothes, we were turned away at the gate. An attractive but severe young lady in black Prada told us we'd need to make an appointment days in advance.

We had dinner that night with Mr. Liu and Mrs. Sung. (I've changed everyone's name. China *does* have a rating of 6 for Civil Liberties.) They were two of the principal Pudong developers, quiet and quietly dressed middle-aged people who had worked in Shanghai's city planning bureaucracy. With that bureaucracy's blessing they set out on their own. They were appalled by the American invasion of Iraq. I was jet-lagged and a bit drunk, but I did my best to make a case for U.S. actions, ending, a bit lamely, with "of course it's too bad to have a war."

"Not too bad," said Mrs. Sung.

"Too *expensive*," said Mr. Liu.

With Tom and Mai, I took a train west a couple of hours to Wuxi, a city of nearly five million people that I'd never heard of. It's the size of ten Clevelands. And if you wonder what happened to Cleveland, Wuxi is where it went. Industrial parks spread for miles with neat, sleek, enormous buildings set in swaths of lawn and landscaping—manufacturing sites for Volvo, GE, Panasonic, Sony, Westinghouse, Nikon, Bridgestone, Timkin, Bosch, and The Nature Factory (I'd wondered where they made that).

We were given a city tour by Mr. Chen, a manufacturer of fleece and plush fabrics. He was proud of Wuxi and so proud of his own fabrics that, although he's the CEO of the company, he carries samples in the trunk of his Audi Quattro.

Mr. Chen was born in 1950 and was studying to be an industrial engineer when the Cultural Revolution arrived. He joined the Red Guards.

"Everyone came to their senses when Mao died," he said. "They realized they had no food or anything else and had been just fighting with each other for nine years."

Thereupon Mr. Chen (if there was irony in this, he didn't let on) joined the People's Liberation Army. During clashes with the Russians along the Amur River, he noticed that the Soviet troops were wearing lighter, warmer synthetic fabrics instead of furs. Although he knew nothing about textiles, he used his friendship with some senior officers to get himself assigned to a small research team. When China entered the world economy, so did Mr. Chen. He had permission, encouragement, and perhaps (though he didn't say so) financing from the People's Liberation Army.

Mr. Chen sent us on in his car to Nanjing, to the groundbreaking ceremonies for Tom's ore plant.

Tom took me to a steel mill he used to run. The company that Tom then worked for bought the mill from the Chinese government for one dollar on the understanding that it would be kept in operation. The mill was eventually sold, for considerably more than one dollar, to Mr. Liu and Mrs. Sung.

The mill's 150-pound ex-PLA guard dog, Shasha ("Killer"), was extremely glad to see Tom. So were the employees. Although there were some steel mill employees who presumably wouldn't have been so glad, such as the 200 or 300 "ghost workers" who didn't exist at all and were on the mill's payroll when Tom took over, plus the 2,000 or so workers he'd fired because they didn't do anything. Tom also needed to get rid of the family who had the local "theft rights" to the factory. They once stole a whole railroad train from the mill and would have gotten away with it if trains didn't have tracks that lead directly to them.

"Here's where a guy threw a wrench at me," Tom said as we climbed the tower to the blast furnace.

"What'd you do?"

"I knocked him down the stairs," Tom said. "Rule of law is the cornerstone of capitalism."

Tom's worst problem with the proletariat, however, involved one of his mill hands, who was having an affair with a woman who worked at the chemical factory next door. They conducted their trysts in an electrical equipment closet. Midst throes of passion the mill hand backed into some high-voltage circuitry and fried. (His paramour, with hair a bit more frizzy than is usual in China, survived.) The man's widow then brought her entire ancestral village to block the steel mill's gates. As compensation for her husband's death she demanded his salary in perpetuity, a job for their re-tarded daughter, a new house, the payment of her husband's gambling debts, and that her grandmother be flown to the United States to have her glaucoma treated.

"I had to call in the Communist Party officials," Tom said.

"Did they ship everybody off to prison camp or some-thing?" I asked.

"They didn't do anything. They said it was my problem. I settled with the widow for a couple hundred bucks."

Tom had an assistant in Nanjing, Lilly. She and her parents and siblings had bought a small tea farm, which they planned to subdivide. Tea bush plantings are in tidy rows, like vineyards but leafier and less stalky—more in the realm of Demeter than Dionysus. It was a pretty spot, set between woods and ponds, and in the least pretty part of it was the little brick house of the peasant who'd owned the land. If owned is the word. In China all land belongs to the state, though this doesn't seem to keep anyone from buying and selling it. The house door was ajar, and I walked into the one shabby room. In the middle of the floor were the peasant's muddy rubber boots—right where he'd left them when he bolted for the fleshpots and business opportunities of Nanjing.

I interviewed a senior Party official responsible for planning and development in the region. He insisted on using his own translator instead of Mai, and I had to submit a list of questions beforehand. I made them as anodyne as possible. "What are the future plans for Nanjing's deepwater port facilities?"

I wanted people to babble away undefensively and without constraint. But I hadn't counted on this fellow.

"With gross metropolitan product of 241.3 billion yuan and 14.2 percent per annum growth, versus provincial 13 percent and 9 percent national, we are seventh-ranked city in economic status, fourteenth in revenue, having 5,000 U.S. dollars per capita income, versus provincial 3,380 and 1,600 national, resulting from Nanjing's 9,000 different industrial products in utilization of 45 billion U.S. dollars capital investment from ninety countries and additional 26 billion U.S. dollars contracted," he said, for a start.

I filled eight pages of my reporter's notebook and he never consulted a note of his own.

"We have forty-eight universities in Nanjing," he said. I don't doubt he attended them all. He concluded, at long last, by saying—though I don't think his interpreter did him justice here—"We want to take this opportunity to make China the world's manufacturing basement."

He and I were escorted to a futuristic conference room with built-in microphone modules in front of each high-backed leather and chrome executive swivel chair. There was an air of Intergalactic Council to the setting. Tom, his chief engineers, and, for some reason, myself, were seated on one side. The senior Party official and a number of sophomore and junior Party Officials were on the other. Everyone, including me, had to give a speech about iron ore and progress and friendship and such. I was pleased to be given a seat at the global economic table even if I (like many of globalization's other guests) didn't know what I was doing there.

Then we all went to the banquet hall and got drunk. There were more courses than you could shake a stick at—apt chiché, given the eating utensils of China. The Party officials laughed at my ineptitude. Then abalone was served with proper flatware, and I laughed at their knifing and forking.

You don't sip your drink in China. And after six or eight rounds of *Gan bei* ("Bottoms up"), language barriers disappear. Mr. Feng, sitting next to me, spoke better English than I do anyway. He went to the London School of Economics. He was full of jokes about the government in Beijing, its muddles, and its meddling. These sent the local Party functionaries into helpless laughter. Mr. Feng proposed *Gan bei* after *Gan bei,* pouring and emptying glasses of Scotch. He had the kind of personality—both engaging and disarming—that probably could get you talking to him about anything, if you could get a word in edgewise.

Promptly at ten the Party members left. Tom and Mai and I saw them to the banquet hall door as their drivers, one after another, pulled up in black cars.

"They used to have Mercedes-Benzes," Tom said. "But then the Central Committee told them they had to use cars made in China." There was a great deal of head-banging and knee-cracking as the Party members clambered into the backseats of locally produced Volkswagens.

"Who is Mr. Feng?" I asked Tom. I examined the business card Mr. Feng had given me, printed with his vague title at a vaguely named trading firm.

"I don't know," Tom said. "But when there's trouble with Communist Party officials—with regulation, bureaucracy, or courts—you go to him. The problem disappears. I think he's secret police."

On Saturday we went to the Nanjing antiques market. "Just walk around," Lilly told me. "Don't look interested. Then come back and tell me what you want. I'll get it—Chinese price."

Mao posters and buttons were gathering dust along with Little Red Books and other Cultural Revolution memorabilia. These used to be popular with the generation of Chinese young enough to think of Mao as funny. But the next generation doesn't seem to think of Mao at all.

Mai and I had lunch with Mrs. Ng, whom Mai had known for a dozen years. Mrs. Ng got her start as Mr. Chen's secretary and now owns a clothing factory. We were in a private room at a resort hotel located in the middle of an industrial park. Bridal couples were getting their pictures taken with the factories in the background. Three flags were flying in front of the hotel: China's, America's, and Pepsi's.

"Congratulations on your MBA," Mai said to Mrs. Ng.

"You got an MBA?" I said. "But you already own a clothing factory."

"Most of the students are successful business people," Mrs. Ng said. "They bring real problems to the seminars. The professors are expected to give practical help." And there you have the greatest contrast to the American educational system that can be described in three sentences.

"There are forty-eight universities in Nanjing," Mrs. Ng said.

When we were finishing lunch I mentioned that I didn't have the slightest idea how clothing was made. Mrs. Ng put her afternoon on hold and showed me. Mrs. Ng's driver took us to her twenty-thousand-square-meter fleece fabric plant. We started with the bales of acrylic. (Acrylic comes in bales? But what had I thought? That it came in cans and bottles?) Then we went to the dye vats with the workers all tie-dye-splattered as though they'd been through an accidental American 1960s. The acrylic is spun dry in a leviathan Laundromat. The fibers are made soft and manageable with conditioner, like a bad hair day writ large, and carded and braided into thick rope with machinery from closed U.S. factories.

"I went to North Carolina to see the textile mills," Mrs. Ng said. "But they were all gone."

The ropes traversed the air above the factory floor—a spiderweb from a spider you don't want to meet—and were fed into automated looms, computer programmed to produce patterns with up to six colors of yarn.

Mrs. Ng, in fact, has two factories. The other produces the garments themselves and covers 44,000 square meters. All sorts of cutting and stitching were going on at a speed that left me more confused about how clothes are made than I was before I'd seen it done. One thing that I could tell, however, is that in the garment industry, piecework is not "unskilled labor."

Mrs. Ng's fleeces and fake furs—in pink mink, disco leopard, shearling from sheep on the moons of Jupiter, and so forth—go out to the youth market in England, Europe, and America. As the father of daughters, the price tags made me pre-ticked-off.

"Ralph Lauren?" said Mai, who'd been talking to Mrs. Ng in incomprehensible female shorthand.

"Not innovative enough," Mrs. Ng said.

The next day Tom had to go back to work in Hong Kong. Mai and I went on to Huzhou, to the southeast, halfway between Nanjing and the sea. Mr. Wu, who runs a woolen mill there, sent a car 230 kilometers to pick us up. And a wonderful car it was, a perfectly restored 1958 Cadillac limousine. We traveled on a new turnpike with rest stops indistinguishable from those in the United States, except for the police walking around the parking lots writing down license plate numbers.

At the border between Jiansu and Zhejiang provinces there was a long line of trucks on the shoulder. "They are waiting for the weigh station officials to take a nap," said our driver.

We toured Mr. Wu's woolen mill, which looks like the nineteenth-century New England woolen mill in the photograph that's always trotted out when the subject of child labor is mentioned—the picture of the thin, sad, patched little girl handling spindles. But in Mr. Wu's mill the little girl is plump, smiling, neatly dressed, and a grown woman. Also, there's fluorescent lighting.

Then we met with Mr. Wu, a formidably undislikable man who's almost as voluble as the Nanjing senior Party official, though with ideas instead of numbers. He took us to his showroom, as modern and stark as any in Milan. The wool coats of the next season were on display. We promised secrecy. But now it can be told. The "must" color of 2007 is burnt ocher.

Then we went to Mr. Wu's conference room, as modern and stark as any in Milan. "China was very smart to follow Mr. Deng," Mr. Wu said. I expected a paean to Deng Xiaoping's combination of Marxist discipline and capitalist growth, but I'm not sure that's what I got. "Because, now," Mr. Wu continued, "whatever Italians can produce, we can produce. Please write that these products are not a threat to the United States. They are a threat to Italians."

Mr. Wu said he was glad to be talking to an author. He had wanted to be an author himself. But he didn't get into the university, because of the Cultural Revolution. He was sent to repair diesel engines on farm equipment instead. He said he believed a good author could be both a good entrepreneur and a good politician.

When the open-door policy began, Mr. Wu got a job as a worker in this very mill. He was promoted to supervisor, then to deputy manager, then general manager, deputy director, and now president and CEO.

"My position in textiles is a bit like yours in writing," Mr. Wu said. This was serious flattery. I think. "Yours is like a boutique product," he continued.

Mr. Wu said that he believed American authors write very fine articles. He'd read one article when he was young that quoted Richard Nixon. "Nixon said something that influenced me a lot. Nixon went to Moscow and gave a speech at the airport that was very good. Nixon said, 'I understand the USSR is a very great country. I come to visit by means of peace. I understand that other means do not work.'"

Mr. Wu said that when he heard that I was an author, he thought of how many things there are to tell the American people. "Tell them," he said, "that of the whole world's GDP, the U.S. has one-third.* Send a message to President Bush that China is *not* dumping things on people. America's policy is leading China to follow the same path as America. U.S. is like a tour guide.

"A lot of things we can learn from America," Mr. Wu said. "Overall we have a lot of people, but our foundation is not quite steady yet. The way we are fighting with America

* Well, not quite, but one takes Mr. Wu's point.

worries me. We need your help. We need your help to solve the problem in Taiwan.

"At the moment," he went on, "China is very stable. The people are happy with their life." He cited Deng Xiaoping's slogan: *Growth is the only reason.* "People support this policy. We have no reason to fight the U.S. We have our own internal problems to work out. For the time being we sell you a lot of products. We want to buy your high-tech products. But you won't sell. *And* it's damn expensive."

Mr. Wu said to me, "You have a responsibility. Not all of Americans can come to China to find out what China is all about. Edgar Snow was the first guy to tell the world about the communist military and the U.S. help in the war against Japan. Maybe you can be the twenty-first-century Edgar Snow and change the opinion of the American people about the Chinese."

Mr. Wu had gone to America some years before. "I had a very good impression," he said, "especially the Twin Towers. When bin Laden hit the towers I said, 'He's a bad guy.'"

Mr. Wu saw his first Cadillac in America and said to himself, "I want a car like that." Then he was in Taiwan at the Chiang Kai-shek memorial, and the tour guide said Chiang loved to ride in Cadillacs.

"We are going for democracy," Mr. Wu said. "Please send the message. Russia had to go through a revolution. We are moving gradually. The American people should take time to understand. On surface we are socialist. Underneath we are capitalist. During the cold war there were lots of struggles, lots of revolutions. China's was the only successful one. We accept America as a great country. President Washington was a great president and led the country to where it is today. The policy of America is correct. But every country has its own situation. You can't use your country as a standard for other people. You love the people and peace. This is the right policy."

Mr. Wu summed up: "You have the patience. We have the confidence."

I had a headache—Nixon, Deng, Edgar Snow, Chiang Kai-shek's Cadillac, George Washington, and I'm almost certain it's supposed to be the Chinese who are patient and the Americans who are confident. Mr. Wu did, however, have one clear piece of advice: "America shouldn't have too many policies."

Mr. Wu took us to dinner with his wife, eldest daughter, and son-in-law. As was the case with several other wealthy people I met in China, Mr. Wu seated his driver and his assistants at the table with his family and his guests. They seemed to be expected to join in the conversation and, except the driver, the toasts.

Mr. Wu's son-in-law was an official in the state-run banking system. I asked him about the number of bad loans that Chinese banks are said to be carrying. "It's not a problem now," he said. "The bad loans were within international standards—only ten percent." (Of course 10 percent of loans going bad would be more than enough to start the U.S. subprime mortgage meltdown a couple of years later.)

Mr. Wu sent Mai and me in his Cadillac to Hangzhou. It's a famous beauty spot on West Lake and, as famous beauty spots go, it's nice enough. Mr. Wu's youngest daughter, Wu Lin, who goes by Linda, has a fashion design company there.

Linda's showroom itself was quite a piece of design, with brutalist concrete stairs, a lit glass disco floor, industrial-chic wrought-iron tables, and neo-Deco porthole windows. The clothes are, Mai testified, fabulous. Linda gave me an apple-green car coat to take home to my wife, who confirmed the fabulousness.

The designs are by Linda's husband, Mike, the only beer-drinking regular guy women's fashion designer I've ever met. Mike wanted to be an industrial engineer and build textile machinery. But in the wake of the Cultural Revolution China's universities were so corrupt that you had to bribe the professors to get into your chosen field. Mike was broke. "Nobody wanted to go into fashion design," he said. Considering the Mao suits that everyone was wearing in those days, no wonder. "It was good luck for me," Mike said.

Linda ran the business side. She was trained as a structural engineer (and would have been an unusually pretty one). "My father wanted me to go into a more serious business," she said. "But in construction you need many people. In fashion you can do it by yourself. This business is very comfortable—no politics."

We went to dinner at a pavilion on West Lake and talked about what Katie Holmes could possibly see in Tom Cruise. Katie is from my hometown, Toledo, Ohio. Linda and Mike were suitably impressed by the fact. "I don't understand this Scientology," Mike said.

I floundered around for an explanation.

"It's American Falun Gong," said Mai.

I watched CNN on television in the hotel room that night. There were brief, almost random-seeming blackouts of things the Chinese government didn't want seen. A whole segment on U.S. criticism of Hu Jintao's trade policies went missing. But I knew all about it because the government censors neglected to delete the caption crawling across the bottom of the screen.

Mai and I flew to Xi'an, deep in north-central China. Printed on the airplane's seat backs, in Chinese, was "Empty space for advertising awaiting you." On our paper coffee cups was "Advertising space available." We were met at the airport by two assistants to Mr. Tian, a manufacturer of coke fuel for blast furnaces. He'd been the main supplier of the mill Tom had run. The assistants wore identical perfectly tailored banker gray chalk-stripe suits.

We were taken to a long, large, and hilarious lunch that went on until there was only an hour's respite before a long, large, and hilarious dinner. The Chinese like beer, wine, whiskey, and their throat-searing *maotai* sorghum brandy. And they serve all of them at once.

The next morning, a little shaky, we went to see the terra-cotta warriors guarding the tomb of the Emperor Qinshihung. Seven or eight thousand of them have been discovered so far. It's said that no two of them are alike, but I wouldn't swear to that in court. What these clay soldiers were all supposed to be doing makes the tomb one of the world's great monuments to "Huh?"

Less mysterious was the peasant who stumbled into the tomb chamber while digging a well in 1974. He was sitting in the gift shop signing copies of the book written about his find—a prosperous-looking old man.

This emperor is revered for uniting China, never mind his policy errors such as purges, massacres, and book burnings, not to mention the expense to taxpayers of having eight thousand terra-cotta warriors made to order.

Mr. Tian was as mildly interested in these as I was. "How much bituminous coal do you use to make your coke, and how much anthracite?" I asked him. (Toledo is not only the birthplace of Katie Holmes; it's also the world's largest soft coal port. When I was a boy an east wind would carry the tarry stink of coke furnaces all over town.)

"Ah," said Mr. Tian, "'fat coal' and 'thin coal,' mixed at 1,200 degrees Fahrenheit." The moment I showed an interest in coal, Mr. Tian told his driver to take us hundreds of kilometers up the Yellow River valley into northern Shaanxi province to see his new coke plant.

We were getting toward Inner Mongolia and the Great Wall. In the hills and canyons of this part of China, the "open door" has barely creaked. Except for the occasional high-tension wires and the pavement beneath our wheels we saw what Marco Polo saw. And how poor the Italy of the thirteenth century must have been that Marco was impressed. The land was terraced to a fare-thee-well. Only on perfectly vertical surfaces had the farmers despaired of cultivation. Crops ran up to the very gravestones. The power from the power lines didn't reach the tiny villages; nor did the pavement or any water pipes. I saw very few animals—no wild ones or any wilderness in which they could live, and not many sheep, goats, pigs, or cows, either. Average annual income here is $415. When the peasants leave to go work in the cities they're called "foreign labor."

This is where Mr. Tian came from. He was born in 1964, the youngest of six children. When he was still a teenager he had an idea to import new kinds of vegetables that could be grown for bigger profits. But he was ahead of his time and was made to study electrical engineering. Although "electrical engineering" is more what Mao, rather than an American, would call being taught to run a movie projector. Anyway, Mr. Tian worked as a movie projectionist and waited for opportunity. After the Open Door came into effect, he started a business trading steel.

"The policy at that time," Mr. Tian said, "was a 'Dual Rail System.'" If you wanted to do something commercial privately, you had to have something to back you up, owned by the government, on the industrial side. The government encouraged contracting with government factories. This didn't work. Government factories didn't produce according to the market. Instead of contracting with a government factory I decided to build my own factory."

"And this was more efficient?" I asked.

Mr. Tian looked at me as if, despite my interest in coal and coke, I might be an idiot after all. "Of course," he said.

When he'd been contracting with government factories he'd learned a lot—by negative example—about how to run a factory. Then he set out to learn about economics. While he was running a trading business and building a factory he was also, like Mrs. Ng in Nanjing, going to college. "There are more than fifty universities in Xi'an," Mr. Tian said. Evenings and weekends he attended what he called "training classes," not only in economics but in basic accounting, marketing, and management. "The cost was a few thousand yuan," he said—about $400. "All the students were businessmen," Mr. Tian said.

The demand for steel was strong, but Mr. Tian shifted his business to coke. Shaanxi province has no iron ore, and Xi'an's steel industry is not well developed, but the region is full of coal to make coke to make steel.

Mr. Tian's coke plant was near China's principal coal mines. The mines look every bit as dangerous as they sound in the continual news reports of death and disaster inside them. Between two of these ominous holes in the ground sat the coke furnace. It was hell's own house trailer, a hot, black, smoking oblong the length of a football field and as tall as the top of the goalposts.

Coke is to coal as charcoal is to wood. Great piles of coal were being fed into the furnace on conveyor belts. There, over the course of twelve hours, the heat of the burning coal itself will turn the coal to coke.

Personally, I considered the coke furnace to be a thrilling piece of machinery. Mr. Tian and his construction crew had built it themselves from scratch. And it smelled like home. The men handling the coal hoppers and balancing precariously on the tailgates of the enormous dump trucks looked pleased with themselves. It made me want to grab a hard hat and get the kind of job where I could throw wrenches at people.

Mr. Tian and I went back to the office and talked with his foreman about coal. Going by the expression of catatonic boredom on Mai's face as she translated, I'll spare the reader.

On the way back to Xi'an I asked Mr. Tian how he'd gotten capital to go into business in the first place. "I needed a guarantor," he said, "someone who was in private enterprise. I had a friend with a company. But, to be honest, at that time it wasn't too difficult to get a loan."

"So it's harder to get started now," I said.

"Yes," Mr. Tian said. "Banks are more straight with loans." A nice turn of phrase, which Mai said she translated literally. But a certain amount of bending had been worthwhile with Mr. Tian. Perhaps Mr. Wu's son-in-law was wiser than I thought in his sangfroid about China's state bank loans.

Mr. Tian said his family had not been affected by the Cultural Revolution, because his father was a peasant and a Party member.

I had been under an impression that the Cultural Revolution had ruined everyone's life. Of course in a nation of a billion people, this can't have been exactly right, any more than Freedom House can be exactly right about China's static freedoms. Mr. Tian thought that some damage had been done by the Cultural Revolution but that the Red Guards were not 100 percent wrong. "During that time," he said, "the people who got criticized were not good people. They were lazy people, people who did wrong to people, right-wingers."

I wondered what he meant by that last term. Mr. Tian was himself a "capitalist roader" and from all I could see he was committed to his route.

"There were factions of Red Guards fighting in Xi'an," he continued. "During the development of the country at that time, it was needed—Red Guards criticizing each other. Criticism was needed. Development wasn't getting far. We were under the pressure from foreign control."

Again I couldn't tell what he meant. American control? Russian control? The control of foreign Marxist thought? "Foreign" is a broad term in China. But I didn't want to interrupt. I'd never heard the Cultural Revolution defended before.

"The country was poor as hell," Mr. Tian said. "We had to come out from this prospect."

Mai and I flew south to Yichang on the Yangtze. Here we'd take a break from my commerce and industry tour and go on a four-day river cruise through the Three Gorges to

Chongqing. A friend of Mai's, Mrs. Han, drove us upriver in her Mitsubishi SUV, to the dock by the Three Gorges Dam where the cruise boat was moored.

Mrs. Han was an executive at the government-owned electric company. She said she didn't want to take a chance on working for a private firm. Government jobs are more stable, though the wages are lower. But her young son was lonely, and if she had another kid she'd lose her job because of the government's one-child policy.

Mr. Tian has several children and five siblings, and Tom's assistant Lilly is one of four. I'd asked Lilly if her parents had gotten in trouble for violating the birth control laws. She giggled and said, "Oh, you know . . ."

"Oh, you know" in China means, "Who you know."

I asked Mrs. Han if the Three Gorges Dam was the ecological disaster that the ecological types say it is, even though the dam's hydroelectric turbines are supposed to produce all sorts of electricity and no greenhouse gases.

Mrs. Han said, "The economy is helped a lot by the dam's infrastructure. But one million people had to move. The farmers are reassigned to be factory workers, and it is not their background. They are living worse than before. But the flooding used to be terrible. There are advantages and disadvantages. It is changing animal life. A lot of historical sites are gone. The farmers are losing good soil by the river."

Mrs. Han was not exactly a spokesperson for central planning.

There are more than thirty million people in Chongqing (or Chungking, as it used to be)—a whole Canada in the space of a Los Angeles. China provides a lot of material for such

statistical tropes, which are supposed to say something mean-
ingful about China, until we try to figure out what that
meaning is.

Mrs. Xia, who runs a franchise business to set people
up in the garment trades, sent her car and driver through
this mob to the boat docks. Mai and I took the car to the
villa that had been General Joseph "Vinegar Joe" Stilwell's
HQ when Chungking was the Kuomintang capital during
World War II. A huge photo of Chiang Kai-shek graced the
front hall. I expressed my surprise to the docent. "We have
to respect history," she said.

We went to dinner with Mrs. Xia and her husband and
Mr. Kang, who runs what is in effect a Chinese Wal-Mart, a
combined department store and supermarket that does 6.4
billion yuan in annual business and produces over 1 billion
yuan in after-tax profits. Mr. Xia is an important something
(I didn't quite catch what and maybe wasn't meant to) in
the Chongqing Communist Party.

Mrs. Xia was fashion-forward, her colors and patterns
and makeup merrily clashing away. Mr. Xia was in an anonymous gray suit. And Mr. Kang had muscles bulging out of
his sport clothes. He looked like a younger Jackie Chan.

Mr. Kang gave me a management lecture straight from
the New York Times' "Business, How-To, and Miscellaneous"
best-seller list. He told me it was important that information
and understanding be shared by all levels of employees in
a company. "And," he added, "that goes for countries, too.

"We are proud of ourselves nowadays," Mr. Kang said.
"I think America believes China is a worthy competitor."
He said that clothing, food, shelter, and transportation are
well taken care of in China. Now everyone wants to travel.
He urged the United States to open its travel market. But he

said it was no longer so important for kids to study abroad. Mr. Xia said that Chinese industrial ownership was "thirty percent private, thirty percent government, thirty percent overseas, and ten percent by the people."

Mr. Kang, like Mao, was from Hunan. He studied business and, after graduating from college, was sent to Chongqing as a government department store manager. "I missed my family," he said. "I could have gone back to live under the shelter of my parents. But here if I succeeded it would be my own accomplishment. I wanted to prove I could do it. For ten years life was very simple, nothing exciting. I kept looking for new things, kept learning. Life is very fair to everybody. If you fail, don't get upset. If you succeed, don't be proud. Character and goal are very important, and persistence. You have to look to details and you will get to big business later. Once you achieve that you should look for something higher. You should be a responsible person."

I managed to interrupt and ask him how he got started. Business was bad at the government department store, so Mr. Kang and two of the other managers went to the government and said that they thought they could do a better job themselves. The government agreed to let them try. They opened their own branch of the government store and made seven million yuan the first year. Now they run the whole chain and own 30 percent of it.

"Does the department store have more competition these days?" I asked.

"Very big competition," said Mr. Kang. "Competition is good. No competition, no growth. I love competition. It makes me excited to go for the fight."

Mr. Xia said, "He's full of confidence."

Mr. Kang said that he hoped by the time he retired his stores would be everywhere in China.

"Even the central government," Mr. Xia said, "is emphasizing that people are the most important."

"I have full confidence in China," said Mr. Kang. "We have to be patriotic." Then, making a leap I didn't really follow, he said, "I support George Bush. He is very frank. Very sincere. But I would ask Bush one thing—to solve the Taiwan problem."

Mrs. Xia started as a seamstress. But she always admired entrepreneurs. "After I'd had a baby," she said, "I thought I should follow my goal to do achievement in life." She took a job as a salesperson at a clothing store even though this paid less than being a garment worker. She wanted to see how the business worked. She borrowed twenty-thousand yuan (about $2,500) and on this slim capital started her own clothing line. By the end of the second year it had almost four million yuan in sales volume. Then she began franchising her business.

"The government is very supportive of what I'm doing," she said. "They gave me a three hundred thousand yuan bonus for helping to solve their unemployment problems." Now she's organizing an "industrial city" for garment manufacturing.

"I have a very great achievement feeling," Mrs. Xia said. "But I have also lost things. I slept two or three hours a night. I lost my husband because I wasn't spending enough time with him. I took my child and had nothing. Then, while I was experiencing my toughest times, I met Mr. Xia. He gave me great support. He was a university lecturer who got promoted to the Chongqing Committee. I have gone through my problems. I have proved myself. I was selected to the provincial assembly and am giving back to society.

Also, I got the support and approval of government. But my corporation is all myself. Because of my high achievement I make my family very happy."

We took a stroll through the center of the city so that Ms. Xia could show me the Party's aptly named Big Hall, built in Bolshevik baroque in 1956 and one of the ten largest buildings in Asia.

"We are learning from American marketing culture," Ms. Xia said. "But we can't learn everything, because the culture is different."

Across from the Big Hall was a monument to the Three Gorges Dam. In a contrast of style with its neighbor this monument consisted of piles of ten-foot-high pyramidal concrete anchors used to keep eroding soil from washing away, interspersed with enormous tires from earth-moving equipment.

"The water won't actually rise much in Chongqing," Mr. Xia said.

Between the monument and the Big Hall was a square almost as expansive as Tiananmen in Beijing. When Mai and I were back in Hong Kong, I mentioned to Tom that the whole time we'd been on the mainland I'd hardly heard the Tiananmen massacre of 1989 mentioned.

"That's no surprise," Tom said. "Tiananmen Square is where the abdication of the last emperor was proclaimed in 1912. It's where the student demonstrations, which led to the formation of the Chinese Communist Party, were held in 1919. It's where the Japanese occupation government announced its East Asia Co-Prosperity Sphere, where Mao declared victory over the Kuomintang in 1949, and where a million Red Guards swore loyalty to Mao during the Cultural Revolution. When the Chinese see a bunch of people gathering in Tiananmen Square, they don't get all warm and fuzzy the way we do. The Chinese think, 'Here we go again.'"

Mai and I flew to Guangzhou (Canton, as it was known for centuries). We stayed with Mai's friend Qing and her husband, Phillip. Phillip had been a museum curator in the United States. He moved to China to restore the antique furniture that had been wrecked and neglected by the communists and to build reproductions using the original types of wood, tools, and finishes. He showed me through his workshop, where he also runs a training program for young Chinese cabinetmakers.

"After a couple of generations when no one cared about craftsmanship," Phillip said, "the craftsmanship is stunning." I watched a young man making an intricate dovetail with a hatchet—the kind of hatchet that was featured in 1940's movie serials about Tong Wars.

Phillip said, "There is, however, a Chinese tendency to do things the hard way."

Qing's father, Mr. Zhao, is one of the last surviving veterans of the Long March of 1934–1935, when the communists escaped encirclement by Kuomintang forces and regrouped to fight both Chiang Kai-shek and the Japanese.

Mr. and Mrs. Zhao came to lunch at their daughter's house. They were full of a rare good cheer of old age. When Qing introduced me as an American, Mr. Zhao laughed and said, "Bush is thinking too much—about Iraq, Iran, Afghanistan, North Korea. He should think less!"

Mr. Zhao was familiar with the costs of excess theory. He and his wife had been upper-level Party officials in Guangzhou. When Qing was a girl the Cultural Revolution had come. She'd told me how everything had gone away—her parents' jobs; the family's house; their food, clothes, and privileges. Mr. and Mrs. Zhao had been subjected to "criticism," as it was so coyly called. "But," Qing had said, "like a kid, I kind of enjoyed the excitement—all of us living in one room and the fighting in the streets."

Mr. Zhao had joined the revolution in 1932, when he was twelve. He belonged to a Communist Party Boy Scout–like organization. He was sixteen when the Long March began. He was one of the "Little Red Devils" who accompanied the troops. He went with the Fourth Red Army led by Zhang Guotao, Mao's more sensible rival for Party leadership. Mr. Zhao did not seem bitter that Mao had won out, or about the Red Guards, or even at Chiang Kai-shek's Kuomintang troops. "We tried to go to Yunnan to fight the Japanese," he said, "but had to fight the Kuomintang first to get there." Then the Kuomintang sent them material for the war against Japan. "And," Mr. Zhao laughed, "we used it to fight the Kuomintang later."

He was, however, still mad at the Japanese. "They had the 'Three Policies,'" he said. "'Burn everything. Rob everything. Kill everything.' Totally unhuman."

"The Japanese people are good people, but their leaders are not," said Mrs. Zhao, soothingly.

Mr. Zhao started out with the Fourth Army taking care of the horses, but was promoted to radio operator. He fought the Japanese for eight years. The Fourth Army crossed the measureless grasslands of western Szechwan three times. The plateau is so full of mire and free of landmarks that the only way they could keep their units together was to spread sideways from horizon to horizon and go forward in a single rank. Even mounted soldiers sank, sometimes horse and all.

They starved until they ate their leather belts. When they finally found some potatoes, one potato filled them so much they were sick. The Fourth Army started the Long March 100,000 strong. Only 25,000 were left at the end. And when they'd reached a mountain fastness—not far from where Mr. Tian's coke furnace is today—they were surrounded by the Japanese. They escaped thanks to the leadership of Peng Dehuai, the best of the Long March military commanders. Some of the women cadres were pregnant and made it down the mountain by holding onto the tails of horses. Other women crawled into baskets and rolled down. Mr. Zhao was assigned to take care of Peng's wife. He was given two bullets: one for himself, because he knew the radio codes; and one for Mrs. Peng. "People like us could not be caught," Mr. Zhao said.

Peng Dehuai would lead the Chinese troops in the Korean War and then be purged by Mao and beaten by the Red Guards, 130 times, until he died.

"Dad," said Qing, "A lot of this stuff I've never heard you talk about before."

Mr. Zhao smiled with the pleasure of being an octogenarian and still able to surprise. Deng Xiaoping had restored Mr. and Mrs. Zhao to their Party posts, but they'd retired in the middle 1980s. "I consider myself very lucky to have survived," Mr. Zhao said. "After the fight with the Kuomintang, when the Communist Party was in charge, I got a lot of benefits from the Communist Party, the opportunity to study." He met Mrs. Zhao at the Party School in Beijing in 1950.

Mr. Zhao was not quite sure what he thought about all the economic development. "He has opened his mind a little bit about money," said Mrs. Zhao. "This is good for his physical and mental health. He's not sure if things are good or bad, but he doesn't talk too much—doesn't argue or criticize."

"I get good Party benefits," Mr. Zhao said. "The organization gives me care and concern. The family is more or less not a big problem." He winked at Phillip. "I feel I have accomplished my wishes. All the children are fifty years old, so I don't have to worry. Now I'm eighty-six. It's wonderful. After that it doesn't matter how long I live. There is a government resort we go to every year. We've built strong relationships there. Right now I have no other wish. If I want to have another meal I go ahead and have it. My only worry is if my wife falls or gets ill. Then she can't take care of me! I am slightly selfish!"

10

SIDE TRIP UP THE YANGTZE

June 2006

❖

It was déjà vu like I'd never seen before. The cliff walls rose from the Yangtze River with a shockingly familiar exoticism. For two and a half millennia China's artists have been inspired by the Yangtze's Three Gorges. And I suddenly understood the improbable, fantastic imagination of Chinese artists. It turns out they're just copying. The crackle-glaze boulder shapes, the crinkum-crankum ledges, the skewed pagoda silhouettes of the mountains belonged to no Occidental geography. Crevice-rooted trees grew branches in chinoiserie decorative curves. Noodle-thin waterfalls splashed columns of calligraphy patterns beside scenery half-emphasized and half-obscured by a feng shui of mist. And in the narrow, crooked alley of sky above the canyons cirrocumulus clouds formed into the endless loops and curlicues of an imperial dragon's butt. Here was every Chinese landscape-painting scroll rolled, as it were, into one.

This is to take nothing away from Chinese art. The average Qing dynasty daub still knocks a Monet into the water lily pond. But bad news for painters: China's government has built the largest dam in the world. The Three Gorges are filling up. Artists will need shorter scrolls.

The Three Gorges Dam was begun in 1993, and the last batch of concrete had been poured in May 2006—a month before my visit. The water level behind the dam had already risen two hundred feet. But, in past flood seasons, the Yangtze sometimes flowed that high. It would be the next hundred feet of water, rising gradually for three years, that would swamp the panorama, plus temples, tombs, and archaeological sites, not to mention 13 cities, 140 towns, and 1,352 villages. *Jamais* replaces *déjà* in the *vue*.

Sanxia ("Three Gorges," as the Three Gorges are prosaically called in Mandarin) is the notch the Yangtze has cut through the mountains on the eastern rim of the Szechwan basin. The gorges are six hundred miles inland from the Shanghai region at the Yangtze's mouth, where China doesn't look Chinese at all. Rapid economic development has made it look like everything on earth.

The city of Yichang, below the Three Gorges Dam, didn't look Chinese, either. That is, it looked Communist Chinese, a remnant of the Maoist love affair with concrete. It's a colorless sprawl of clunky bunkers, the factories indistinguishable from the housing. The East is Gray, or used to be. And cracked and flaking.

But economic development has come to the Yichang region as well. A part of it is Victoria Cruises, an American-managed company that runs a handsome fleet of riverboats on the Yangtze. The ships are new, each with about 100 cabins and staterooms ranging in size from the more than grand to the more than adequate. Our ship, the *Victoria Star,* was fifty feet at the beam and 277 feet long, displaced 46,000 tons, and had all the swabbed decks, shiny brass, and polished teak that nautical pretensions could demand. Hatches in the starboard bulkheads led to private deck space. (I'm too nautically pretentious to say that there were sliding doors to the balconies.)

Traveling by river in China is preferable to traveling by road. The English drive on the left. The Americans drive on the right. The Chinese respect both customs. Mai and I arrived on the quay to find that there were a thousand stone steps between us and the *Victoria Star*'s gangplank. An actual coolie appeared with the kind of bamboo shoulder pole that I thought no longer existed except on the printed chintz of fancy upholstery fabrics. He slung our suitcases on each end and, balancing luggage that weighed as much as he did, skittered downstairs for two U.S. dollars. We were piped on board by the *Victoria Star*'s band to the tune of what, given the band's minor difficulties with Western melody, might be called "Yangtze Doodle Dandy."

In the morning we embarked for the Gezhou Dam, 8,579 feet long, 154 feet high, and completed in 1988. This was an earlier effort to tame the Yangtze. The dam's concrete looked homemade. As the father of three young children I am, perforce, a fan of handicrafts, but not when they're 154 feet tall.

The *Victoria Star* filled the ship lock with maybe eighteen inches to spare on either side. Later I talked to Captain Gong Ju Chen, a mast-straight and very captain-like fellow. Maybe, thanks to Mai's fluency and understanding of cultural nuance, I could catch the real flavor of Yangtze shipping, plumb its lore. An Asian *Life on the Mississippi*? With 1.3 billion potential readers?

Me: "How do you maneuver such a large ship into such a narrow lock?"

Captain: "Very carefully."

We docked twenty-some miles above the Gezhou Dam at Sandouping and got on buses for a tour of the Three Gorges Dam. There was bus tour guide humor: "We call this a 'dam day.' Hope you do not think I am 'worst dam guide.'"

Three Gorges was more professionally constructed than Gezhou, and it had better be. By 2009 the dam would be holding back more than ten trillion gallons of water. Any slipup will make New Orleans after Katrina look as if somebody didn't close the shower curtain. The dam lacks the high swoop of dramatic grandeur that "man's harnessing of a mighty river" calls to mind. No Margaret Bourke White photograph could turn it into a *Life* magazine cover. It's a blocky structure blocking a gorge. The fluted downstream wall makes it slightly (and it is to be hoped not ominously) resemble a squat World Trade Tower. The thing *is* big, bus tour guide pun big—496 feet high and almost 1½ miles long. Apparently there was plenty of concrete left over from the Maoist romance. Thirty-five million cubic yards of it were used.

Two shipping lanes are built into the dam. Passage requires the traverse of five locks. There's also a ship elevator able to lift boats and the water they float in, sixteen thousand tons in all. Or, rather, it's unable to lift them. After the ship elevator was built, it was discovered that no cable ever made is strong enough to hoist it. "German company is being consulted," said our guide.

China being still, officially, a communist country, in a confused way, mixed signals abound. There are old socialist touches. On top of the monumental dam is a monument to the dam. It's in the middle of a parking lot full of Buicks, VWs, and Audis. Next to that is a Buddhist garden, perfect for meditation except that loudspeakers in the shrubbery are playing pop songs.

The garden, however, *was* perfect for a confused meditation on the Three Gorges Dam. It is vehemently condemned by nosy, whining world-savers. It is fervently defended by Communist central planners. These are two groups that are usually reliably wrong. And they both have good arguments.

Environmentalists say the dam will destroy the Yangtze's environment, trapping pollutants and waste in a four hundred-mile-long reservoir, which will become what that backpacking world-savers' bible, the *Lonely Planet* guide, calls "the largest toilet in the world." Having spent some time peering into the Yangtze's waters, both up- and downstream from Three Gorges, I don't think the Ty-D-Bol Man's job could get any harder.

According to a Chinese government brochure, the dam has technology allowing it to "store clear water and discharge muddy water." But, in the matter of technology and the Chinese government, there is that phone call to the Association of Big, Thick Cable Manufacturers that no one made before the ship elevator was built.

Ecologists say the dam will destroy the Yangtze's ecology. Species such as the Yangtze sturgeon will become extinct. There are no fish ladders at Three Gorges (or fish elevators, either). Fish won't be able to get upriver.

But, the central planners point out, boats will. The dam project clears navigational hazards for a thousand miles inland on a river with so much shipping that it has to be guided from what, at first glance, seem to be misplaced airport control towers along its banks. "There is disadvantage to the fish," our guide said. "We have built an institute to solve this."

Human rights activists say the rights of 1.5 million humans are being violated by forced relocations from the Yangtze valley. The central planners say the main purpose of the dam is to control the flooding in that valley. The worst flood in recent history, in 1931, terminally violated the human rights of the 3 million humans who died.

The dam's twenty-six hydroelectric turbines are expected to supply 50 percent of China's electrical power, although that is communist central planner math. Maybe the central planners haven't looked at how Beijing, Shanghai, and Guangzhou are lit up these days. They may be thinking of 50 percent of electrical power when it was generated from the static of Mao jacket sleeves as Little Red Books were waved in the air.

The Chinese government also intends, our tour bus guide told us, to build an "International Holiday Center" at the dam. Perfect for people who plan vacations to Southern California to see the freeway intersections. Or maybe members of the World Wildlife Fund will stop by on an Indignation Tour.

But the central planners may be more right about resort possibilities than they realize. To keep the riverbanks from eroding as the water rises, thousands of acres of concrete have been poured directly over the contours of the ground. The Yangtze is lined for miles with rolling, bucking, precipitously inclined pavement. It is a skateboard paradise, a thrasher's Eden. Forget the Beijing Olympics and make Three Gorges the permanent home of the X-Games.

Anyway, the dam is built. The tour bus guide said, "Three Gorges are beautiful, but I do not think that living your whole life in a gorge is a beautiful thing."

That afternoon the *Victoria Star* entered the gorges. They stretch for 120 miles. During the next twenty-four hours we traveled though the Chinese puzzle boxes of the Xiling Gorge; between the Great Wall-dwarfing 2,800-foot cliffs of the Wu Gorge, and up the five-mile opium pipe of the Qutang Gorge, where the river narrows to 330 feet.

I consult my notes. There aren't any. I had meant to write a magazine travel piece, but I stood at the rail, reporter's spiral-bound pad in hand, and couldn't look away long enough to get the cap off my pen. As the bus tour guide had implied, the Three Gorges are too beautiful to make a living in.

Sometimes I would step back inside the parlor deck, where the *Victoria Star*'s private river guide, Michael Yang, was giving a lively commentary to the passengers. Who were not so lively. There were three package tours of Europeans on board, mostly British of a certain age and divided between the earnestly dull and the simply dull. The earnestly dull were deeply concerned with the fate of the Yangtze sturgeon. The simply dull were like a house party in an English murder mystery without the murder. Thankfully, there were two very jolly Australian couples for Mai and me to dine with at the "Independent Tourists" table. The cruise would have been more fun if it had been filled with Chinese—*Gan bei!*

The Victoria Line is popular with Mainlanders, but they prefer the downstream trip through the gorges. It's one day shorter and lets them have their vacation more quickly.

"Everyone on the Mainland is in a hurry, even with their leisure," Mai said.

Coming back from the dam tour I'd overheard two of the simply dull tourists discuss the social and economic transformation of twenty-first-century China:

First tourist: "We did Shanghai, Beijing, and Xi'an eight years ago."

Second tourist: "Must have changed."

First tourist: "Traffic is horrendous."

On the parlor deck Michael was pointing to a rock formation off the port bow. It's known as "Rhinoceros Admiring the Moon." The Chinese have a different way of looking at things. I would have said Bill Clinton giving Newt Gingrich the finger.

"What of the fate of the Yangtze sturgeon?" asked an earnestly dull tourist.

Between the Xiling and Wu gorges was the birthplace of the poet Qu Yuan (330–295 BC). Michael said that Qu Yuan drowned himself in despair over the political policies of the Qin dynasty, and the event is still celebrated all over China in the annual Dragon Boat Festival. Anybody who's met a political-activist suicidal poet knows how the Chinese feel. But it seems harsh to make a national holiday out of it.

There are many important temples, pagodas, and places of historical interest along the Three Gorges. But I was having a bachelor-party-at-a-strip-club experience—intrigued with appearances and not too interested in listening to histories. I liked Michael's commentary best when fog descended on the river and visibility was zero. Then Michael, who knew exactly where the boat was, would continue his discourse anyway. It took me back to the days of being stoned in the college classroom, the prof going on in a very entertaining manner about the significance of something—maybe the poetry of Qu Yuan—that was totally lost on me.

It was hard to sleep at night. I kept getting up to watch the ship's spotlights sweep the sides of the gorges. The beams glittered in the skinny, fitful waterfalls—reminding one of the Mandate of Heaven pouring approval on Chinese economic reforms, perhaps, or of prostate problems, depending on one's age. Along the river verge the lights shone on gutter-wide towpaths that had been cut into the cliffs in the days when Yangtze riverboats were roped to naked laborers and yanked upstream. Another picturesque feature of the Three Gorges was about to be sacrificed to ecologically woeful navigational channels and their polluting boat engines—doubtless to the applause of a million ghosts of Yangtze boatmen.

When we emerged from the Three Gorges, Michael had everyone go to the stern and hold up a ten-yuan bill. There, on the back, were two almost conjoined mountains, like a pair of rugged Yangtze boatman hands about to clap, forming the gate to the Qutang Gorge. The engraving looked exactly like what we saw from the taffrail, but slightly taller because it was engraved a while ago. Mai said, "Mainlanders would be keeping their eye on the ten yuan."

After a fortnight spent in a hurry with those Mainlanders, three days and four nights on the *Victoria Star* were welcome. The ship has no casino, video game room, hot tub, wave pool, climbing wall, jogging track, or character actors in mouse costumes. The cruise directors, Jenny Goodman and Bob Shigo, actually gave useful directions instead of taking the *Poseidon* movie approach and turning the boat upside down to keep everyone busy.

Jenny speaks Mandarin and looks like a lass in a Robert Burns ballad. The combination startles people when she travels in hinterland China, she said, as if George W. Bush all of a sudden spoke English. The food—Western and Chinese—was good. The Chinese food was somewhat tame, which was also good. With the Mainland entrepreneurs and industrialists I had learned that duck tongue is good. Duck foot webs less so. Donkey meat tastes like corned beef. And chicken stomach boiled in hot pepper oil tastes better than it looks (and hardly could do otherwise). It was a relief to lift the lid of a serving platter and discover lo mein.

Mai practiced tai chi, got a foot massage, flew kites from the top deck (losing one in a suspension bridge that has loomed lower since the Yangtze began to rise), and went to a cabaret show of traditional Chinese music and folk dance with Broadway improvements by former drama major Bob Shigo. I made the acquaintance of highly skilled chief bar steward Ricky Yang.

And I stared at the shore. The ordinary sights of the Yangtze are, in some ways, more extraordinary than the Three Gorges. The terracing on the hillsides could have been done for artistic effect. But it wasn't. The stones of the walls were carried and stacked, generation after generation, to make, in some places, no more than a flower box of level soil for crops. The overwhelming economic power that is modern China all grew from these narrow margins of substance. And the economic power is visible everywhere. A fishing village of six stone hovels, without a road in or any sign of plumbing, displayed five satellite dishes.

It came so close to not happening. I noticed that, in the highlands above the terraced farms, the forest hills of the Yangtze valley lacked something. Forests. I asked Michael about this.

"They were cut down to feed backyard blast furnaces during Mao's attempt to match U.S. steel production." Michael, who had been born in 1977, after China began to become normal, gave a baffled shrug.

Sometimes, however, China's embrace of market economics manifests itself oddly. On a brief shore excursion, a government-employed guide told us that a street parade was an advertisement for a furniture store sale. Mai, reading the parade banners, said it was an announcement of an upcoming Communist Party celebration.

We stopped at a 3,000-year-old town that was being slowly inundated. Another government guide brought us ashore. She took us to a new town that had been constructed to house the residents of the drowning town. The buildings were made of concrete and topped with fiberglass panels imitating roof tiles. There was an industrial area to provide jobs for displaced farmers. Nothing was in it except stacks of waste paper. "The industry is recycling," said the government guide.

We went ashore at Fengdu to visit Snowy Jade Cave, which occupies the whole interior of a small peak. Traveling through it is like an inside-out mountain hike. The cave was discovered in 1994, opened to the public in 2003, and appears in none of the guidebooks I've consulted. This is just as well. The cave contains millions of calcite crystals. There's a certain kind of American tourist who believes that crystals make something special happen, and I don't want to be near that tourist when every one of those special things starts to happen to her all at once.

The interior is, as the cave's name implies, white. The crystals are formed into Sun Valley mogul fields, peels of New England birch bark, backyard clothesline bedsheet billows, Dairy Queen swirls, diner mugs, urinals, and stalactites and stalagmites ranging in shape from ash blond bang fringe to obscene personal vibrator. Obviously Snowy Jade Cave had been discovered too late to inspire China the way Three Gorges did. The names in the cave had a Chinese touch, however. One scenic area was called "Improve Your Life."

On the day before our boat reached Chongqing, David gave a talk for the passengers titled "Modern China." But what he told was the story of his family. During the Cultural Revolution his parents had made, between them, fifty yuan a month. There was rationing until 1990. When David was born, the most expensive item in his house was a radio.

After the "open door," farmers were able to lease their land from the government in return for 15 to 20 percent of their harvest. David's father was a truck driver. He leased a truck from the government trucking company for 10 percent of his profits. Before Deng's reforms, all jobs had been assigned by the government, for life. "Everything was assured," David said, not reassuringly.

David's father was scolded by his mother for leasing the truck. But in five years his father had made 80,000 yuan (about $10,000), which, in those days, was enough to buy a house. The largest banknote then in circulation was the ten-yuan bill. His father brought his profits home in a large sack. David's mother thought he'd stolen the money. They had the first refrigerator in their neighborhood.

David went away to boarding school. He came home to Chongqing after a year, and so much building had been done that he couldn't find his house.

His parents lost everything in the Asian market crash of 1989. "They moved to a small village," David said, "and worked all day and all night to start a tourist resort. Now they are prosperous again."

David was educated as a chemical engineer. He was working as a guide while he waited for a visa to get his PhD in the United States. After September 11, 2001, visas became hard to obtain.

"China's economic and social progress has been very fast," David said. "Just five years ago I was amazed by the cleanliness and order of Singapore." He said that in the 1980s if a family had a watch, a bicycle, and a sewing machine, they were considered rich. In the 1990s it was a color TV, a refrigerator, and air-conditioning. Now it's a car, a computer, and a mobile phone.

David explained, "The Chinese constitution is somewhat similar to that in the United States. The highest authority is the Party." He then offered to take questions.

Among the tourists was a British woman who looked as though she cut her own hair. "But who's been *hurt* by all this economic development?" she asked.

David was puzzled. At a loss for an answer, he said, "Even ten years ago we had spy machines in all four-star hotels."

"If the old days were so terrible," said the British woman, "why the long queue at Mao's tomb?"

I resisted the temptation to say, "They're making sure he's dead."

"Some older people," David said, "are nostalgic for the Mao era. They have the grudge in their hearts about the big differences of income. And about the insecurity. Old people say, 'You cannot use the money of tomorrow.'"

"What are the main problems facing China over the next ten years?" asked another, less irritating tourist.

"The income gap," David said. "The next five-year plan has to increase the living standards of farmers, eliminate the agricultural tax, and provide incentives for people to stay in the countryside."

"What about all those rich farmers on their private plots?" said the woman who cut her own hair.

"The outsides of the houses may be nice," David said, "but the insides are empty."

"And what about all these beggars we see?" said the woman.

"We used to arrest them," David said. "But Western countries criticized China's human rights."

"What will China's geopolitical role be in the future?" asked a third tourist, who looked smug about coming up with such a BBC interview of a question, albeit posed to a twenty-nine-year-old chemical engineer.

"In the long run, a very neutral role," David said. "China tries to be as humble as possible. There is the Taiwan issue and the Tibet issue, both handled very well by the government. But all these issues are basically economic concerns. If China's economy climbs, all these problems will disappear."

"I was thinking," said the DIY haircut woman to a promenade deck full of people who wished she'd quit doing so, "that there are some world problems that need handling by China, such as global warming."

"We want to have more friends," David said.

"But what about global warming?" the woman said.

"We just want to be loved," David said and looked at his watch and announced with relief that time was up.

11

A Horse of a Different Color

Kyrgyzstan, July 2006

❖

I was standing in the stirrups, stretched over the horse's neck. The reins were clenched in my teeth. I was gripping the mane with my left hand and swinging a quirt with my right, whipping the horse up a steep, grassy mountainside. There were hundreds of feet to climb to the top and a thousand feet to fall to the bottom. It had been raining all night. The grass was slick. Hooves churned. Forelegs milled in the air. Hind legs buckled. The horse was on the verge of flipping backward. And that was the least of my worries.

In the first place, I don't know how to ride. I can't ride a horse up a mountain. I can barely ride a horse at all. Until shortly before doing this impression of Sir Edmund Hillary as Roy Rogers my equestrian experience was limited to going around in circles to calliope music on a pony with a pole through its middle.

In the second place, I was somewhere in Kyrgyzstan. Not only didn't I know what I was doing, I didn't know where I was doing it. And I wasn't in the Westernized, cosmopolitan part of Kyrgyzstan—such as it is—with hospitals and ambulances. I was in the part with no roads, electricity, or cell towers. A satellite phone was in my saddlebag, but I couldn't get a satellite connection. Even by the standards of outer space Kyrgyzstan is remote. If something happened to my horse it would be shot. For me, the medical treatment wouldn't be that sophisticated.

Furthermore, there were blond hairs all over my clothes and luggage. How would I explain this to my redheaded wife? I had a love affair in Kyrgyzstan. Not only that, but with a male. His legs are so beautiful. And he has four of them.

All this began—as such things tend to—over a couple of drinks. I was having them in London with the fellow who had taken me to the Exmoor stag hunt, Adrian Dangar, whose surname is only slightly misspelled. Adrian, besides writing about hunting for *The Field*, runs a small, bespoke travel agency called Wild and Exotic. I was telling him that I planned to go to Kyrgyzstan, one of the former Soviet Republics in Central Asia, to write about how, or if, democracy is developing in places with no democratic traditions. This seemed a safer way to investigate the question than going to Fallujah. I was wrong.

"Funny you should mention Kyrgyzstan," Adrian said. He told me that he was organizing a horse trek across the mountains there in the coming summer, with Alexandra Tolstoy and her husband Shamil Galimzyanov. Alexandra is the great-great-great- (give or take a great-) niece of the author. Though English by birth, she speaks Russian and lives in Moscow. Shamil is a Tartar from Uzbekistan whose family has been training horses since horses were the diminutive things with toes that we see in the Natural History Museum evolution exhibit. Shamil knows the region. So does Alexandra. A few years earlier, she and three girlfriends from college had retraced the Silk Road on horses and camels for five thousand miles from Merve, near the Iranian border, to where Mr. Tian and I had been bored by the terra-cotta warriors in Xi'an, China.

"We'll have a great trip," said Adrian. "Come along. You'll see parts of Kyrgyzstan the Kyrgyz haven't seen."

"But I can't ride," I said.

Adrian has been riding since he was in utero. He's been Master of Hounds for several particularly neck-breaking fox-hunts. He's ridden across the Serengeti and over the Andes. "Nonsense," said Adrian, "a horse trek is just backpacking on someone else's back."

Back home in New Hampshire, I told Mrs. O., "I'm taking a horse trek across the mountains of Kyrgyzstan."

"No you're not," she said.

"Come on," I said, "it's not like the mountains of Kyrgyzstan are such a dangerous place."

"No," she said.

"I've been to lots more dangerous places than that."

"No."

"I was a war correspondent for twenty years, for gosh sake."

"You've *been* to a war," Mrs. O. said. "You've never *been* on a horse."

She relented, at last, on the condition that I take some months of riding lessons. This I dutifully did, from a dressage instructor in an indoor ring atop horses named Elmer's and Mucilage. And that is how I ended up in a tent camp in the heights of Central Asia. Kyrgyzstan is a nation the size of South Dakota that's all but lost among the Tian Shan Mountains, the "Heavenly Mountains," that divide China from the trans-Ural steppes. It is north of Kashmir and Afghanistan, beyond the Hindu Kush and the Pamirs, past what even Alexander the Great considered worth conquering. The country is, or might as well be, the "Kafiristan" of Kipling's *The Man Who Would Be King*. (And, over the next two weeks, my horse would try to crown me with any number of tree branches overhanging our trail.)

A fellow named Djuman Kul, who looked like Genghis Khan and was wearing a felt hat as tall and amazing and elaborately embroidered as anything the Pope dons for Easter, was choosing my mount from a herd of wild Kyrgyz horses. They were wild enough, at least, that nobody had bothered to name them. I had been picturing something on the order of a shaggy little Mongolian pony that would let my feet drag reassuringly on the ground. But these horses were fifteen hands high. That is, they were five feet tall at the shoulder, and thin and bony-headed as fashion models but sinewy like a California governor left outdoors to eat grass all winter. And the horses were stallions, with Floyd Landis levels of testosterone. Like Floyd and Tour de France officials, they were kicking and biting each other.

Djuman Kul led the lone palomino forward. He told me in Kyrgyz, Shamil translating, "This horse is strong, but kind." I wish I had not overheard Djuman telling each of the other trekkers, "This horse is strong, but kind."

I dubbed the horse "Trigger" and hopped aboard. There is a trick to this. You turn the left stirrup backward, place your left foot in it, and, springing with your right leg, swing yourself up so that you . . . slam your whole body smack into the side of the horse. Shamil helped me up. I had an excellent, if precarious, view of Kyrgyzstan. It looks like the American West. Not the dry-gulch western-movie American West (for which I had, without long underwear or adequate rain gear, packed), but the whole West—purple mountain majesties, fruited plain, noble forest spires, canyons as grand as grand can be, packed into one place with about as much sign of human habitation as Lewis and Clark saw. (Sacagawea, please go to the satellite phone.) It would have taken my breath away if I hadn't been too scared to breathe.

Not that Trigger was giving me much to be scared of. Per my riding lessons, I assumed a proper "seat," placing the balls of my feet on the stirrup treads with heels down and foot, hip, and shoulder aligned. I held the reins low, threaded over my pinkies and up into my hands, "carried like two flutes of champagne," as I'd been taught. I felt for the correct gentle contact with Trigger's bit. I applied a subtle pressure with my lower legs and gave the reins the requisite slight flick. Trigger stood there. I tried all of the above a little more forcefully. Trigger stood there. I tried more forcefully yet. Trigger stood even more there. Everyone else was riding away. Djuman Kul handed me the quirt. He pantomimed a ferocious Patrick O'Brian novel shipboard lashing. It is one thing to beat a miscreant of about one's own size who has been firmly tied to a mast. Beating a nine-hundred-pound critter that could buck you to China and run over there before you landed and then kick and bite you is another. Trigger received the sort of spanking that a six-year-old gets on a birthday. He ambled off, thankfully in the right direction.

That direction was onto the middle of a bridge over a small but Napoleonic mountain stream. I'd noticed the bridge earlier. What I'd noticed was that I wouldn't care to cross it on foot. It was made of several logs arranged like the losing turn in a game of pick-up-sticks. I cared a lot less to cross it on six feet, two of which had come out of their stirrups.

"Trust the horse!" Shamil yelled. "Let the horse do the thinking!" It is an experience, the first time you stake your life on a brain to which you wouldn't assign the simplest task such as keeping the lawn short without destroying the flower beds. I endured a mortal version of the fear my wife feels whenever she sends me to the grocery store.

On the other side of the bridge was a cliff, 500 or 600 feet high. The horses went right up it. Trigger found each tiny notch in the rocks by feeling around with his horseshoe as though he were typing a blog. Then, when his posting seemed to be put strongly enough—DEATH TO REPUBLICANS ON OUR BACKS!!!—he pressed "send." I didn't die, because there was always one part of Trigger that held still enough for desperate clinging to. His withers were firmly planted as his backside fluttered in the breeze. His loins stayed solid while everything up front gyrated in scree.

Trigger climbed hoof over hoof. And here was an excellent idea for yuppie sports marketing, if I survived—horseback climbing walls. Indoor facilities could be built in Southampton, Palm Beach, and Beverly Hills. A rider and steed, in one big harness, are top-roped and belayed by a dozen climbing coaches. "Left rear hoof on the red hoofhold," shout the climbing coaches. "Hook your right front pastern over the blue. Don't look down!"

Or up. Because at the top of the cliff there was no top. There was more and steeper cliff. Traversing this was a path the width of a dollar bill. The landscape had been turned 180 degrees. The horizon was viewed by ignoring the climbing coaches' advice.

I don't own a hunting cap, and I wasn't about to show up in Kyrgyzstan wearing my daughter Poppet's pink Hello Kitty bicycle helmet. Now I saw that headgear was necessary only to preserve enough dental work to make the corpse identifiable. I rode with one stirrup banging against the cliff face like the knell of doom and the other a footrest on the bottomless pit. Beyond the cliff were forest glades of the kind that, at an American ski resort, put an end to Michael Kennedy. He had it easy. The wet clay of Kyrgyzstan is deeper and faster than Rocky Mountain powder and Trigger is more self-willed than any pair of Rossignols. We went up, which was bad; then down, which was worse. Plummeting through a boulder-choked chute, there were times when Trigger was beyond vertical, when my boot heels were out past his ears, and, no, I didn't need a haircut, that was Trigger's tail flopping over my face.

After nine hours we reached camp on the Arkit Sai River. Shamil and Alexandra have two seven-ton, six-wheel-drive ex-military trucks, surplus from the Soviet Union's Afghan war. One is rigged as a kitchen and the other carries the gear. A camp staff of half a dozen rode in these down logging skids and sheep tracks and across country to meet us each evening. Tents were up. Latrines had been dug. A table was set with a line of vodka bottles down the middle. A local lamb was roasting. And I was splayed on the riverbank reveling in my good fortune. I wasn't dead. And I wasn't dead in a magnificent place. And I magnificently wasn't dead among splendid people, whom I've neglected to mention because I've been too busy being scared.

There were fourteen of us, including Adrian, Alexandra, and Shamil. It was such an intrepid cast of characters on such a thrilling journey during which I got beaten to such a pulp that introductions may be made according to pulp thriller conventions.

Andrew Stott—senior executive for Nestlé, UK, master of campcraft and avid foxhunter, who could lead a charge of the Light Brigade every bit as well as he charges (quite reasonably) for coffee and cocoa.

Ettie Boyd—superb athlete and corporate headhunter, the horsewoman who saved me from my own "Into the Valley of Death" experience by tactfully pointing out that whipping Trigger while yanking on his reins was making him as confused and stupid as . . .

"Me?" I suggested.

Claire Morrissey—North Dublin colleen possessed of the Irish way with dumb animals, sits on a horse with the same aplomb and authority as Tip O'Neill sat in the House of Representatives (but cuts a much finer figure).

Jennie Crohill—Norfolk countrywoman and seemingly an unassuming farm inspector for the British government but actually the hero who shot the last feral coypu in England. (It would sound more thrillerish if I left that unexplained, but a coypu is a nutria, a giant South American aquatic rat with a body two feet long. They were raised for fur, escaped, bred in the wild, and were playing merry hell with the Norfolk marshes.)

Bahar Ghaffari—exquisite Persian miniature, looks nineteen but is a Master of the Universe investment banker in Hong Kong, juggling equity derivatives so complex they make Alan Greenspan's head throb.

Camilla Coventry—raised on a ranch in Australia, but she and Crocodile Dundee are from the outback the way

Lauren Bacall and Mel Brooks are from New York. Studied theater and can produce and direct *Annie Get Your Gun* and do all the stunt work, too.

Jean Baptiste Oldenhove de Guertechin and Gaetane Schaeken Willemaers, Belgians with educations as elaborate as their names. He a global management consultant with a degree in civil engineering and an MBA from the Wharton School of Business. She an international finance lawyer and the former counsel to Belgium's minister of foreign affairs. They are on their honeymoon.

Harold van Lier—another Belgian, a movie producer turned hotelier because guest towels have more wit than entertainment executives. He is on his honeymoon as well.

Emily—Harold's beautiful English bride, a relief worker specializing in third world sanitation problems (of which I was one at the moment). She has given up international aid work to come to the aid of, well, people such as ourselves, at the Grand Hotel des Bains in Brittany. As the name implies, it has plenty of sanitation.

"In your article about Kyrgyzstan," said Harold, "you must not use the term 'tour group.' It is as if we had silly Americans along in pink Hello Kitty bicycle helmets. None of us would ever join a 'tour group.' We are a 'tour horde.' We will sweep down upon Samarkand, Bukhara, and Tashkent and pillage . . . since some of us are Belgians . . . their chocolate and lace."

"You had better have another vodka," said Shamil, "because tomorrow the riding becomes difficult."

We rode through the village of Kizel Kel', where Djuman Kul and our horses were from. A lone electrical wire and a notional road connected it to the world. And even this much civilization the Kyrgyz leave, spring through fall, to graze their herds in the mountain pastures. Stay-behind women and kids and the eighty-year-old blacksmith (who had "about forty" grandchildren) came out to say hello and feed us apricot jam.

We went up into a cartoon-beautiful forest, climbing with animation—feature-length animation—through Shrek-colored fern glades with sunlight pixilating in the tree leaves. Irish Claire herself had never seen anything so green. We emerged to a view that looked even less real and left me faint with a wish that it weren't. We were on a scythe blade of a ridge, thousands of feet in the air. Snowcapped mountains loomed, but they loomed below us. We could see rivers, in extremely small scale—threads of blue monofilament. Mile-wide turquoise lakes glinted minutely, beads lost in a shag rug. We were at the top of the Chakal range of the Tian Shan, above everything.

Above almost everything. Obese thunderheads material-ized on top of us. Jovian flatulence erupted. The sky would have been black if it hadn't been bright orange with lightning. Gaetane's curly hair stood on end, making a nimbus three times the size of her head.

"It is an interesting phenomenon, an effect of ioniza-tion," said Jean Baptiste.

"You look like Medusa," said Harold, "But much prettier, of course, and without the snakes."

"@#$%! GET DOWN!" screamed the nervous person from a country with frequently toasted golfers.

The best we could do was a thicket of stunted trees with a lush undergrowth of stinging nettles. It poured. It blew. The temperature dropped thirty degrees. The nettles were enjoyed by the horses. Ettie and Claire got under their mounts. This, if you've seen a horse relieve itself, was a calculated risk of a worse wetting. Camilla said, "I know what—*The Sound of Music*."

> The hills are alive with the sound of . . .
> KA-BOOM
> "@#$%! GET DOWN!"
> Doe, a deer, a female deer,
> Ray, a drop of golden . . .
> KA-BOOM
> "@#$%! GET DOWN!"

The path descending from the ridge was washed out. Shamil found a crevasse leading . . . somewhere. It was too muck-sunk and brush-filled to ride. We had to lead the horses. An enormous creature is behind you, threatening at every moment to add the mud luge to the list of Olympic equestrian events. Taking a fall on a horse is just a matter of one's own slobby body mass index hitting the ground. It is not to be compared to having a horse take a fall on you. There were places where leading was impossible. We had to jump and slide on our own, then call the horses like dogs, asking them to perform stunts that Lassie would have left Timmy down the well rather than attempt.

Trigger, who'd shown no previous inclination to obey, or even notice me, turned petlike and followed with pup-pyish devotion. The crevasse opened into a gorge, and the gorge opened into a canyon, and once, when he and I were stuck on a ledge, Trigger gave me a little nudge away from the abyss. (Though it's possible Trigger is dyslexic and was pushing in the wrong direction.)

The rain kept on and so did we, in a trail-breaking slog until our spirits had descended as far as we had. And there on the canyon floor were our trucks. Using a frayed old Soviet topo map, drivers Valeri and Andrei had guessed where we might emerge. The cook, Tyota Vera, and her helpers Nadia and Lyuda had a hot meal ready. A tarp was stretched over the table.

"You had better have another vodka," said Shamil, "because tomorrow the riding becomes *very* difficult."

It did. We climbed three thousand feet up a slope like a graph of crude oil prices to have lunch with the shepherds of Kizel Kel'. Their yurts are streamlined for the mountain winds—Airstream trailers made of felt but with more spacious and contemporary open-plan interiors. We ate yogurt and little balls of goat cheese fermented in burlap sacks hanging outside the yurts, and we drank the whey that dripped from the bags. The Kyrgyz bring little with them by way of provisions except their livestock. There was a lot of gawking, mostly from the Kyrgyz. Being nomads, they are tourists themselves, and after a wet night in camp and a long ride we were a sight. Emily, with her background in relief work, was relieved to see no relief was needed. The camp's three families and their fourteen kids were smiling and fit. Either they lead much healthier lives than we do or they roll their sick down the hill. I imagined the size of the saddlebag needed to carry to the mountaintop my family's sunblock, bug spray, asthma inhalers, orthodontic retainers, vitamins, dietary supplements, and bottles of shampoo and conditioner formulated to correct high-altitude dryness and split ends. We rode out through a canyon with walls that will dwarf the luxury resort that is

going to be built there someday, through clouds of blue but-
terflies where the parking lot will be, and under a natural
bridge, naming rights available. The striated sediment in the
sandstone cliffs had been bent by mountain-building into a
gargantuan taffy pull. Owners of leisure homes will be sure
to frame this view in the master suite's Palladian window.
Hundreds of feet up, ibex skittered across the openings of
unexplored caves. Unexplored cave tours at ten, noon, and
two. Shamil, reconnoitering the canyon on foot a month before, had seen a Tian Shan brown bear and the spoor of a
snow leopard. Call the concierge for safari bus reservations.

"This canyon is one vast herbaceous border," said Jennie, standing by a yard-wide clump of irises and naming a
dozen other plants. "All these have to be so carefully tended
in England, and here they just grow."

"Herbaceous Boarder" is a clever name for the upscale
bed-and-breakfast that will cater to the more ecologically
conscious visitors.

We vilified progress all the way to our cooked meal, distilled
beverages, and double-walled synthetic fabric expedition
tents. The river at the mouth of the canyon will survive—
sweeping fly fishermen and kayakers straight to perdition.
We tried to take a bath in it. Ettie had the guts to go first,
lowering herself into water the temperature of decompressing
Freon and being beaten by the roil of pebbles in the current.
"Yow," she said, "this is worse than a spa. You know, there
are people who pay thousands for things like this."

"Us among them," said Andrew.

We rode for two days through the Chakal Range's
meadow fairways, not one of them less than a par ninety-nine.

Golf would be a more exciting sport if it had been invented by the Kyrgyz instead of the Scots. You'd hit a horse instead of a ball, and it would be you that would wind up in a hole in the ground, six feet under if you weren't careful.

Being careful on Trigger wasn't hard. The other horses were galloping around. But for Trigger, as for many of the world's great beauties, being beautiful was a career. Doing anything else that he didn't have to was a waste of his valuable talents. Trigger would go where the other horses went with a Kate Moss vacuity. But out on his own, on open ground, he'd prance, flare his nostrils, arch his neck nobly, gaze at the fields of wildflowers, and eat them.

Trigger and I were married or—I'll have to check the laws of Kyrgyzstan on this point—joined in a civil union. Anyway, there I was on top going "Yes, Dear." Of course the other riders were skilled and accomplished. Although some of them said they weren't.

"I haven't ridden since I was a kid," said Bahar.

"Bahar," I said, "you are a kid."

"Jean Baptiste has spent only two hours before on a horse," said Gaetane. Jean Baptiste blushed with modest embarrassment at being a natural athlete and quick study.

I am neither. And I'm pushing sixty with a short stick. And I was chafed and sore in surprising places. In unsurprising places, too. Do not wear jeans on a hundred-some-mile ride through a graduate course in geography. You'll have permanent raised seams right where Levis do. But I was also rubbed raw in my belly button from where the pommel of my saddle had dug into my gut going uphill and in the small of my back from where the saddle's cantle had caught me going down hill, and the bottoms of my feet ached because I'd been unconsciously pressing on the stirrups with an old automobile driver's instinctive hope that one of these things was the brake. Yet every night, after half a bottle of vodka or so, I became a brilliant rider. In fact we all became quite brilliant. Adrian and Andrew figured out exactly where Osama bin Laden was hiding—in the unexplored cave where we'd seen the ibex. They trapped him there, put an end to terrorism, and forged a lasting peace in the Middle East, although they were somewhat fuzzy on the details the next morning.

Jean Baptiste discovered that he could play the guitar. Camilla staged a production of *Grease*, complete with choreography.

> Tell me more. Tell me more.
> Did you get sore, of course?
> Tell me more. Tell me more.
> Like, does he have a horse?

A week into our trip we awoke below the mountain where Trigger would experience near-gymnastics. It stood at the end of a seemingly endless meadow. Blossoms of clouds drifted down from its peak on sunbeam stems arranged in an urn of celadon mist, or something like that. It was a scene to make me wax as florid as the nature poets of the Romantic era, although, compared with Kyrgyzstan, the Lake District of England looks like a rest stop on I-95.

"I think," said Shamil, "when we die this is what we see."

I'm glad to say that's not the means by which I saw it. Trigger didn't tumble. We made it to the top. And I could ride Trigger after all. He didn't change direction with leg pressure. It was reins on his neck that made him turn. The quirt was no punishment, just a memo from middle management. I couldn't post; that is, I couldn't rise rhythmically with Trigger's trot. His gait was too much like a hoppy toad's. But I could canter if I kept my mind—and my behind—on what I was doing.

And I had other epiphanies up there. I wasn't scared. I was still a coward, but I'd run out of fear. The grassy slope had depleted my proven reserves of trepidation, vast as they were. I'd also run out of adjectives. My ability to describe was as exhausted as my ability to worry. We went through a bunch-of-superlatives countryside down to a highly-evocative-metaphor valley and on to our campsite that was, oh, darn nice.

Except there was no camp. The trucks and the crew weren't there. The rain had been causing landslides on their routes. Alexandra's horse had gone lame and she'd ridden in one of the trucks that day. Shamil was grim with worry. It began to rain again. There was no food. Our canteens were empty. The sun set. It rained harder.

Miles down the valley was a government forestry station, intermittently occupied. The horses were worn out. We hobbled them and began to walk. The flashlights were with the camping gear.

Hours later, at that moment in a cold, wet, dark hike to an uncertain destination when the soul cries out for a cozy office cubicle and a job making unsolicited dinnertime phone calls asking people to switch their cable service, Alexandra appeared. Indeed there had been a landslide. She and the camp staff carried the supplies and equipment to the other side of the debris. They commandeered a logging truck. And they brought, thank God, the vodka.

The weather cleared the next day and so, eventually, did our heads. We rode on through mountains, fields, and forests. The Mongols and the Huns and Shamil's ancestors must have felt like this. They didn't really mean to overrun the known world and sack it; they just didn't want to stop riding.

And one afternoon on the banks of a lake called the Sary Chelek, the "Golden Bowl," I galloped Trigger. A real gallop with all hooves—and not me!—launched in the air. We ran for a mile and a half along the lakeside. We were a centaur. Trigger was Pegasus. I was Alexander on Bucephalus, conquering Kyrgyzstan after all.

Now I know what it is to be a *chevalier,* to be the Man on Horseback. I'm making the patio into a paddock. I'm building a stable in the garage. I'm getting Trigger a green card. I'm learning to jump so I can go foxhunting. There are plenty of foxes just an hour and a half away in the suburbs of Boston. And a hell of a hunt it will be because every hedge has a swimming pool on the other side. I wear my new jodhpurs around the house, and all that I talk is horse sense.

"One small sore butt for man," says Mrs. O. "One giant pain in the ass for mankind."

12

Sweet-and-Sour Children and
Twice-Fried Parents to Go
Hong Kong, December 2007

Having been a foreign correspondent for many years, I'm used to leaving home. I'm not used to home tagging along after me.

I was invited to give a lecture in Hong Kong.

"Let's take the children," said Mrs. O.

"It's a sixteen-hour plane ride," I said.

"Sixteen hours," said Mrs. O., "equals about one Sunday sleet storm trapped in the house with the kids while you're someplace like Hong Kong."

We'd traveled overseas with the children before. Muffin turned two in Venice. There, in the middle of Saint Mark's Square, a

Japanese tourist lady handed her an open bag of pigeon feed and every feathered rat in Europe descended on the poor tyke. I have mentioned that my wife is afraid of birds. The feeling was mutual after Mrs. O.'s rescue of our daughter in a Burberry-brandishing, Coach bag–slinging, swashbuckling attack on the flock. The Piazza San Marco was cleared of pigeons, maybe for the first time in history. The Japanese tourist lady was also run off.

Then there was the night—the whole night—in a Madrid hotel when Poppet was teething and Muffin was howling in solidarity and Mrs. O. and I were trying to figure out what's Spanish for "warm milk." (*Leche picante* is not it.) But since Buster (our Iraq War baby boom baby) came along, skiing in Ohio and one trip to Disney World were as far as we'd ventured as a family.

The portability of children is not improved by their number, or, for that matter, by their age. Muffin, age ten, was starring in a preview of puberty. The preview had been edited for general audiences—that is, Muffin was experiencing all the moods, manners, and misanthropies of adolescence without (mercifully) the sex, drugs, and rock and roll. On the other hand, Mrs. O. and I were enjoying this about as much as we would have enjoyed adolescence ourselves without the sex, drugs, and rock and roll.

Poppet, seven, was in that excessively imaginative stage of childhood so beloved by children's book authors and so annoying to everyone else. For example, many children are afraid of the dark, but Poppet was also afraid of having a night-light. "Because then the monsters stay awake and crawl out from under the bed, and they want to talk, and I want to be nice to them, but I'm tired." She also had a tendency to burst into tears during random moments of television viewing.

"It's an ad for kitty litter," I'd say.

"People are littering with kitties! Just throwing them out car windows!"

And then there was Buster, three—Bill Clinton in a diaper. He's an almost pathologically friendly child and terribly upbeat but, at three, still in a diaper all day. Airplane toilet changing tables are not built for sturdy three-year-olds or their ham-handed fathers who've had a drink or two. What with getting the changing table down and Buster up and the bulky diaper bag open, Buster and I could spend the whole sixteen-hours wedged inside the airplane toilet.

I tried to have a talk with Buster about being too grown-up to be in a diaper. I said, "Now, how old are you?"

Buster—Clinton-like in his free-and-easy way with his past—said, "I'm five."

"No," I said, "You can't be five. Five-year-olds don't wear diapers."

Buster gave his lip a Clintonian bite, thought for a moment, and said, "I'm six."

The lecture invitation had come by way of our Hong Kong friends Tom and Mai. They race horses and it was International Race Week, with the Hong Kong Jockey Club hosting the best turf-racing horses from all over the world. The Jockey Club runs the horse racing in Hong Kong, and all the betting proceeds go to charity, making the Jockey Club the largest charitable organization in the Special Administrative Region and—thanks to Hong Kong's mania for betting on horses—one of the largest in the world. Various affiliated organizations also hold charity functions during race week. Tom got me to talk to something we'll call "The .50 Caliber

Club," an all-male group of four hundred of the most prominent and drunkest race horse owners in Asia. Every year they
put on an epic five-hour lunch with numberless courses and
bottles to match. What little I know about horses I left, with
a fair amount of hind-end skin, in Kyrgyzstan. But I know a
lot about drinking in the daytime. (The speech apparently
was well received, although nobody, me in particular, seems
to remember much about it.)

Cathay Pacific Airways was the principal sponsor of International Race Week. Cathay offered to fly me over, and
gave us a deal on additional seats. For purposes of economiza-
tion we got two seats in business class and a three-seat row
in economy. Muffin and Poppet grabbed business class and
surrendered themselves to the joy of chairs and footrests that
can assume hundreds of positions and an entertainment system chock-full of stuff they aren't allowed to watch at home,
not to mention a magic button that you push and a nice lady
brings you things to eat. Each of our daughters was as happy
as a newly hired CEO in the corporation's Gulfstream G-5.
And I have great expectations for Muffin in this respect. Her
egotism, unwarranted self-assurance, and continual exercise
of pointless willfulness make her into pretty much every boss
I've ever had. Poppet will need to find a different route to
private luxury jet travel. Perhaps her disordered imagination
and romantic notions about actuality can be channeled toward
derivative swaps and collateralized debt obligations.

Poppet can be quite convincing, if you make the mistake
of listening to her. Our flight took us over the north pole.
Poppet went straight to the window, looking for lights from
Santa's house. Never mind that she wasn't in a window seat.
This caused some inconvenience to the person across the
aisle. I went forward to check on the girls and found Poppet

and the businesswoman to whom the window seat had been assigned both earnestly searching the ice pack for evidence of Saint Nick. I tried to extract Poppet.

"No, no," said the businesswoman, "I think I just saw the glimmer from an elf lantern."

As it got toward midnight our time (three drinks and a *New York Times* past the girls' usual march to bed), Muffin and Poppet discovered the lie-flat feature on their seats. This, combined with Cathay's privacy cubicle seat layout, gave the kids ample boudoirs with space for the Serengeti migrations of stuffed animals with which they travel. (Muffin considers herself too old for stuffed animals, but if she gave them up Poppet might enjoy them and that would spoil things for Muffin.) They went to sleep, or what passes for sleep with traveling children, meaning they got up every twenty minutes to make sure their parents weren't enjoying three drinks or getting to read the *New York Times*.

Those parents had Buster between them. Buster disdains stuffed animals and (again like Bill Clinton in Bill's salad days) goes everywhere with a motorcade. He had at least fifty toy cars and trucks in his Speed Racer backpack. I'm glad he's a boy's boy and all, but when I tried to doze off with a semi-tractor trailer stuck in my backrest I did wish he'd get in touch with his feminine side and collect Beanie Babies.

When Buster isn't acting like a politician, he's acting like a large-wheeled vehicle. He guns his engine, grinds his gears, and beeps when he backs up. Having Buster in the next seat is like trying to snooze on a highway yellow line. Finally, Mrs. O. and I lost our supervisory will, and Buster took the off-ramp over my knees. I heard his fire engine siren heading to first class and his ambulance wail coming back toward the galley. Then I fell asleep.

I awoke, I don't know how much later, with no sign of Buster and a cold fear that Cathay Pacific was headed for an emergency landing in the Aleutians, where our family would be arrested for violating the TSA rule against being a pain in the neck. I went on a hasty search. Buster was chatting away to the prettiest of the stewardesses.

"I'm sorry," I said. "Has he been causing a ruckus?"

"Oh, no," the stewardess said. "We told him that the airplane captain ordered no fire engines or ambulances allowed in the aisles, and he quieted right down. Then he went around and introduced himself to everybody, but only to the people who were awake. He didn't bother anyone who was sleeping. He'd ask if they wanted to play with his toy trucks. And, before he wore out his welcome, he'd move on to the next person."

In the due course of a damn long time we landed in Hong Kong. We proceeded down the aisle with two sleepy little girls and the Night Mayor of Cathay Flight 318. Everyone waved to Buster.

"Bye, Buster!"

"So long, Buster!"

"See you later, Buster!"

As soon as jet lag had sufficiently abated, Muffin began lecturing us—and all the Chinese within earshot—about China. "In China they don't have the alphabet," said Muffin. "They have pictures instead. And every picture is a word instead of a lot of letters. For instance that picture." She pointed to a character on a billboard. "You can see that that's the word for snakes and worms fighting over a cabbage."

Poppet began to sniffle. "What if the cabbage gets hurt?"

When I was a foreign correspondent I regarded Hong Kong as "starter Asia," perfect for introducing the Orient to neophytes. Everyone is impressed by how colorful and exotic it is, except it's clean, safe, and it works. However, there is no telling what will impress a family. If any of the kids noticed that they'd gone from rural New Hampshire to a metropolis teeming with millions, they didn't think it was worth mentioning. And Mrs. O. didn't notice that the place is cleaner than our kitchen at home. She began her program of applying antibacterial wipes to every surface on the Asian continent.

Buster was wowed that he could take a taxi without being strapped and buckled into a child seat as if he were going on a doomed Challenger mission. And then, to his immense delight, we encountered his idea of paradise—a traffic jam. "Truck! Car! Truck! Bus! Car! Car! Truck!" noted the observant little fellow.

An ad for Hong Kong Disneyland caught Poppet's eye. She gasped with excitement.

"No!" I said. "We went to Disney World back home. You didn't even like it."

"I felt sorry for the mouse and the duck," Poppet said.

"Why?"

"Because they had people sewn up inside them."

"But, Dad," said Muffin, "this time would be different. See, we fly a million miles, all the way around to the other side of the world. And then we go to someplace that's exactly the same. That would be so cool." The entire travel and tourism industry explained in three sentences.

I knew what would catch my wife's eye. On a trip to the shopping capital of the world she had "accidentally left at home" a suitcase full of the clothes she "needed most" so she "had to" go shopping. Gucci, Dior, Dolce & Gabbana,

Coach, Louis Vuitton, Bulgari—each has a gleaming flagship store in Central. I tried to distract Mrs. O.

"Honey, look up in the sky!" Oops. There was a huge neon Ralph Lauren logo there. "No, look down. The kids might get pushed off the sidewalk! Traffic in Hong Kong is . . ." Screech . . . honk!!!

"Funny Daddy," said Buster as I was almost run over by a bus. My wife slipped from my grasp and ran into Shanghai Tang's, taking all of our credit cards.

With Muffin and Poppet holding onto my blazer pockets I pushed Buster's stroller uphill past the Lau Kwai Fong bar fronts. Mainland China legislates family planning. Hong Kong just lets the impossibility of using a stroller do the trick. I'll never allow anyone to criticize the Americans with Disabilities Act again. There isn't a curb cut anywhere in the Special Administrative Region. And Hong Kong's steepest side streets, such as the one I was on, are, in fact, staircases. Some of the steps are as tall as Hu Jintao. I'd hoist Poppet, prod Muffin, and do a weight lifter's snatch and jerk with Buster in the stroller. Sweat-soaked, winded, and probably (given Shanghai Tang's prices) broke, I reached Ice House Road and the Foreign Correspondents' Club. I had been anchoring the right, rear corner of the bar there intermittently since the late 1980s. I ordered the usual. One of the waiters approached. He asked if the children would like something to eat. The FCC serves food? Who knew?

One thing that Mrs. O. and I have learned about traveling with children is to avoid hotels. There's a cage-like atmosphere to hotel rooms, which brings out the zoo animal and not just in the Allman Brothers Band. You do not want to get to the point where the room service waiter ditches his tray outside the door and runs down the hall heedless of his tip rather than face your kids.

So we rented an apartment in Hong Kong, in a good neighborhood, Happy Valley. The worry was that we'd rented it sight unseen. I have been in Hong Kong apartments so small that you had to open the door to burp. Fortunately, apartment 15A in the Ovoid Tower had two adequate bed-rooms and a reasonably spacious living/dining/stuffed animal corralling/toy truck parking area. Unfortunately, owing to the building's namesake shape, the apartment had a Cessna fuselage form and the only place left to install the kitchen was where the nosewheel ought to be. We could always send out for Chinese.

Being fifteen stories up and in a nose cone pleased the kids. "We can play airplane!" said Poppet. You'd think that after our flight to Hong Kong, playing airplane would be like getting a combat veteran just back from Kandahar to go out for a game of paintball. The apartment also had a view of the Happy Valley racetrack. This was a great tear-saver, since both girls are crazy for horses, and Hong Kong bans children from attending horse races. We could see almost the entire course, with only part of the backstretch obscured by the apartment block next door.

"It's Alpo in the lead coming out of the second turn with Rival gaining on the rail and Purina falling to third. Now they're under Mrs. Woo's clothesline, into the Wong family's front hall, and through Mr. Chung's bedroom. Kibbles and Bits is coming from behind. Gravy Train on the outside into the stretch. And . . . it's Meow Mix by a nose!"

*   *   *

I went to the real races at Happy Valley, and courtesy of
Tom, I was ensconced in the luxury of the owner's suite with
fitted carpet as deep as gambling debts, a buffet that was a
veritable thesaurus entry for good and dictionary definition
of plenty, and drink that flowed like . . . simile fails me due
to drink . . . drink. I was wearing my loud tweeds and the
world-famously ugly FCC club tie and was feeling quite the
sport, aided by the Hong Kong dollar's eight-to-one exchange
rate. I could puff myself up with the pronouncement, "I'm
putting a thousand on this race."

I picked the odds-on favorite to show, a bet that, as
I recall, paid out HK $1,002. Then I put my winnings on
Tom's horse, which came in . . . um . . . somewhat ahead of
the start of the next race.

Meanwhile, Mrs. O., Mai, and the kids went to the Po Lin
monastery on Lan Tau Island to see the Tian Tan Buddha,
the largest bronze casting of its kind in the world. Mai, who
doesn't have kids and hasn't traveled with three of them who
act like miniature Americans, came back looking, shall we say,
sympathetic. Mrs. O. was what she calls "intact." And the children returned glowing from the intense aesthetic experience.

"We had ice cream!" said Poppet.

"Double dip!" said Muffin.

"On my pants!" said Buster, displaying proof that his
deed was as good as his word.

"But what about the Buddha?" I asked.

"The what?" said Muffin.

"You know," I said, "Buddha, the Indian holy man who
founded Buddhism. You went to a Buddhist monastery." (I

thought we were supposed to be worried that American kids were being exposed to too much multiculturalism.) "They had a statue of Buddha. It's really big. What was it like?"

"Really big?" said Muffin.

"We had ice cream!" said Poppet.

"On my pants!" said Buster.

I held out against Hong Kong Disneyland but gave in to the longer-established, less product-placement-infested Ocean Park. It's sort of Six Flags Over Hong Kong. And—considering the Qing dynasty, British, Japanese, British again, Special Administrative District, and, pretenses aside, Communists—six flags is about right. This gave me the opportunity to bore Muffin with some history. And bored she was. The preteen mind has two modes: astounding know-it-all and amazing ignorance. Muffin responded to my pocket lecture on Hong Kong with, "I knew that. I knew that. I knew that. Are Communists the good guys or the bad guys?"

Ocean Park is set atop the coastal cliffs of Aberdeen, on the south side of Hong Kong Island. The amusement complex is reached via a scary Alpine gondola ride with naked rocks and nasty surf beneath it instead of the illusion of cushioning snow. This alarmed us all—enough, I hoped, to quench the children's desire to go on alarming rides. Children do not, however, learn from experience. It may be their best trait. It keeps you from feeling obliged to hang around providing them with experiences all day and lets you send them off to school instead, in the hope they'll learn something that way. And it allows you to be a remarkably grumpy parent, while dragging them around Hong Kong, for example, and still get a good-night hug.

The kids and their parents rode on . . .

"Forget it," said Mrs. O. "I drive them to school every day. That's enough of a thrill ride for me."

The kids and their dad rode on . . . the Vomit Rocket, Coma Comet, Puke Chute, Spin-N-Spew, Nosebleed Express, and Loop-De-La-Defibrillator. In vain I hoped that height restrictions might spare me some of this, at least with Poppet and Buster, but I was on a continent where "You Must Be Taller Than the Clown to Ride" is a profound insult to half the population.

Ocean Park, in the earnest, self-improving Asian manner, has an instructional side to it. Interspersed among the rides were various exhibits focused on ocean life and full of icky undersea creatures, as if I didn't have mal de mer already.

Poppet claimed she could understand what the sharks were saying.

"They're saying they're going to eat you," said Muffin.

"I told them they couldn't," said Poppet complacently. "We're in Hong Kong and they don't know how to use chopsticks."

The particular feature of Ocean Park that the kids liked best was the mainland Chinese. There were tour groups full of them, mostly in late middle age and easy to spot with their off-brand clothing and out-of-town haircuts. Mainland Chinese are the midwesterners of Asia. But these were midwesterners who'd never seen a blond child. The older female tourists descended on our two towheads, Poppet and Buster. They hugged them, posed for pictures with them, ran their fingers through their hair. The kids accepted instant celebrity with composure.

I kept waiting for the Lindsay Lohan behavioral blowback. It never came. Adult celebrities are people who wish they were the center of the universe. This is a wish the child mind has already granted to itself. And I'd expected Muffin to be jealous while the mainlanders fussed over her siblings. Instead, she pulled her Ocean Park cap down over her eyes and hung back demurely. So much the center of the universe is Muffin that she skipped the fame-seeking part and went directly to paparazzi avoidance. Children are actually very interesting. They'd probably be worth reporting on if they got their own country or something.

I took Muffin and Poppet on the tram to Victoria Peak. But they're country kids. They've got a mountain out the back window, and a train runs through the local town. A train going up a mountain is too conceivable. They were fascinated instead by the escalator that runs between Central and Mid-Levels. Where we live it's an hour's drive to an escalator of any kind. And the Mid-Levels escalator is half a mile long. "We should get an escalator instead of a car," said Muffin. "It would help save the planet from having greenhouse gas."

Mrs. O. and Mai went to Mai's dressmaker near the Western Market in the Sheung Wan neighborhood. I was sent off with the kids to get them and my suggestions out of the tailor's shop. Now I had a chance to introduce the children to the real city, engage them with the genuine spirit of the place, get them to understand the idea of Hong Kong. We went shopping.

We went to a "wet market" selling parts of animals that even country kids didn't know existed. We inspected seafood so fresh it seemed—given some chopsticks—at least as likely to eat us as we were to eat it. And we examined vegetable oddities that looked like remains taken from a Roswell, New Mexico, flying saucer crash. We went down alleyways full of thingamajiggers, dofunnies, and jiggumbobs. Buster got a toy taxi and, by way of charades, persuaded the shop owner to let her finger serve as the passenger and be transported all over the countertop. I gave the girls a handful of Hong Kong dollars and sent them into the stores to make their own bargains. Mai had been coaching them in Cantonese.

Everything that makes for a terrible pre-teen—the attitude, the talking back, the eye-rolling, the exasperated sighs—makes for an excellent Hong Kong shopper. That's how shopping is done in Hong Kong. Poppet couldn't quite get the knack of it. But Muffin would flounce into a shop, examine a few items without evident interest, and loudly announce, "*Ho gwai!*" ("Too expensive!")

More than one shopkeeper came out from behind the cash register to embrace her. "You real Hong Kong girl!"

Muffin and Poppet bought Christmas presents for Mom. Back home Mrs. O. would receive, from the Hong Kong Santa, a Tian Tan Buddha snow globe; a pair of embroidered slippers (size 1½); a kite in the shape of, I think, a cockroach; and a paper mobile phone that can be burned on the grave of Mrs. O.'s ancestors so that they'll have cell service in heaven.

I took the kids back to Ovoid Tower to teach them to eat properly with those chopsticks. This is easy, with the help of HK $100 worth of candy. You start with gummy bears. Anyone can pick up a gummy bear with chopsticks. Then you progress to gumdrops, through Hershey Kisses and jelly beans, until you arrive at the ultimate test of skill, the peanut M&M. Dad calls floorsies!

"But what about noodles?" asked Poppet, who, since her talk with the sharks, was taking the subject seriously.

"Oh, even the Chinese can't eat noodles with chopsticks," I said. "Just wait until your mother isn't looking, bring the bowl right up to your face, and shovel the noodles into your mouth like everybody else does." We practiced with Twizzlers.

Mrs. O. came home burdened with packages and also Chinese take-out.

"We're *so* not hungry," said Muffin.

Mrs. O. eyed the candy wrappers covering the apartment floor. "Would that have anything to do with candy?"

"Candy is a state of mind," said Poppet, who seemed to have been absorbing Oriental philosophy.

Tom and Mai had a barbecue on the roof of their apartment building in Wan Chai. I looked at the splendid view and drank. Mrs. O. looked at the all-too-climbable railing around the patio and didn't.

We don't generally—because we're not insane—bring our children to grown-up parties. But Tom and Mai insisted. "The secret to traveling," said Tom, who has spent even more years doing it than I have, "is to bring the party with you." Our little party comported themselves pretty well, ages considered.

Muffin realized that if she carefully refined her sulk, she could do her sulking in front of Tom's wide-screen TV watching Japanese anime while the caterers served her treats.

"Muffin," said Mai, "will make a perfect Tai Tai." (Rich Hong Kong wife.)

Buster attached himself to the best-looking female guest. He jumped into her lap, clasped her hand, and, moving her wrist from first through fourth gears, explained how to use a stick shift. Then he told her everything about ambulances and fire trucks. Mrs. O. tried to shoo him off. He turned and glared and said in a fierce whisper, "Mommy, go away! I'm talking to *she!*"

Poppet, however, was undergoing a homesickness meltdown. It seems that in the congress of plush toys that accompany her everywhere, some key player—perhaps the Speaker of the House Nancy Pelosi stuffed ferret or something—had been left behind in New Hampshire.

When I'd had enough to drink to be under the illusion that things can be explained to children, I called on my old pal (who, sadly, has since died) Hugh Van Es to back me up in my pep talk to the sobbing Poppet.

"I know you're homesick, Honey," I said. "But everybody here's been homesick. We've all spent lots of time away from home. Remember that picture that I showed you in the Foreign Correspondents' Club? The one with the helicopter on top of the building and all the people escaping? Uncle Hugh took that picture. It was in the Vietnam War when the bad guys conquered Saigon, and Uncle Hugh was the only reporter left. Think how homesick he must have been."

"But Uncle Hugh," said Poppet, awash in tears, "you didn't leave your most important stuffed animal at home."

In a day, of course, the homesickness had doubled back on itself. Poppet was weeping about the prospect of leaving Hong Kong. "Because there's no feng shui in New Hampshire."

"Feng shui?" I said.

"Aunt Mai told me all about it. Everything has to be rearranged to make the invisible dragons happy," said Poppet, rearranging her stuffed animals and Buster's trucks and cars. "In Hong Kong *everybody* sees invisible dragons, just like I do!"

Buster came out of the nosewheel kitchen and raced through the bedrooms with his police cruiser PA system blaring. "I live in Honk-Honk! I live in Honk-Honk!" He paused in front of me, bit his lip, and looked serious. "Daddy," he said, "do ladies like diapers?"

"Ladies?"

"Like *she*."

"Your father," I said, "would never claim to be an expert on what women want. But, no, ladies don't like diapers."

And Buster has been, more or less, dry all day ever since—having made a sacrifice of self-restraint for the sake of beauty that puts him one up on Bill Clinton in the moral intelligence department.

Muffin and Mrs. O. returned from shopping. Muffin had discovered an Australian surf-wear shop where the clothing was manufactured to look like it had already been eaten by Poppet's shark with the chopsticks. "I am *so* over New Hampshire," said Muffin.

I was sitting in the FCC with Hugh Van Es. CNN International was broadcasting news about very interesting-looking riots in Indonesia. That and a few drinks were making Hugh and me wax nostalgic about our foreign correspondent careers. The children ate noodles in the approved Chinese fashion. Mrs. O. arrived from Central with more packages. Hugh called for the waiter to bring her a Tai Tai drink and said, "You and the kids seem right at home in Hong Kong."

"P.J. is not," said Mrs. O., "allowed to leave us here."

13

The Big Stick, or Why I Voted for John McCain

USS Theodore Roosevelt, April 2008

❖

Landing on an aircraft carrier is . . .

To begin with, you travel out to the carrier on a powerful, compact, and chunky aircraft—a weight-lifter version of a regional airline turboprop. This is a C-2 Greyhound, named after the wrong dog; C-2 Flying Pit Bull is more like it. In fact what everyone calls the C-2 is the COD. This is an acronym for "Curling the hair Of Dumb reporters," although they tell you it stands for "Carrier Onboard Delivery."

There is only one window in the freight/passenger compartment, and you're nowhere near it. Your seat faces aft. Cabin lighting and noise insulation are absent. The heater is from the parts bin at the Plymouth factory in 1950. You sit reversed in cold, dark cacophony while the airplane maneuvers for what is euphemistically called a "landing." The nearest *land* is 150 miles away. And the plane doesn't land; its tailhook snags a cable on the carrier deck. The effect is of being strapped to an armchair and dropped backward off a balcony onto a patio. There is a fleeting moment of unconsciousness. This is a good thing, as is being far from the window, because what happens next is that the COD reels the hooked cable out the entire length of the carrier deck until a big, fat nothing is between you and a plunge in the ocean, should the hook, cable, or pilot's judgment snap. Then, miraculously, you're still alive.

Landing on an aircraft carrier is the most fun I've ever had with my trousers on.

And the twenty-four hours that I spent aboard the USS *Theodore Roosevelt*—the "Big Stick"—were an equally unalloyed pleasure. I love big, moving machinery. And machinery doesn't get any bigger, or more moving, than a U.S.-flagged nuclear-powered aircraft carrier that's longer than the Empire State Building is tall and has four acres of flight deck. This four acres, if it were a nation, would have the fifth- or sixth-largest air force in the world: eighty-six fixed-wing aircraft plus helicopters.

The *Theodore Roosevelt* and its accompanying cruisers, destroyers, and submarines can blow up most of the military of most of the countries on earth. God has given America a special mission. Russia can barely blow up Chechnya. China can blow up Tibet, maybe, and possibly Taiwan. And the EU can't blow up Liechtenstein. But the USA can blow up . . . Gosh, where to start?

But I didn't visit the *Theodore Roosevelt* just to gush patriotically—although some patriotic gushing was called for in America at the time. And while I'm at it, let me heap praise on the people who arranged and guided my Big Stick tour. I was invited on the "embark" thanks to the kindness of the Honorable William J. (Jim) Haynes, former U.S. Department of Defense general counsel. The trip was arranged by Colonel Kelly Wheaton, senior military assistant to the Acting Department of Defense general counsel, Daniel Dell'Orto; and by Lieutenant Commander Philip Rosi, public affairs officer of the Theodore Roosevelt Carrier Strike Group.

I traveled with the Honorable Mr. Dell'Orto and a group of ten (minus me) Distinguished Visitors. On board we met people more distinguished yet, including Captain C. L. Wheeler, commanding officer of the *Theodore Roosevelt*; Rear Admiral Frank C. Pandolfe, commander of the Theodore Roosevelt Carrier Strike Group; and Command Master Chief Petty Officer Chris Engles, who—as anyone with experience in or of the Navy knows (my dad was a chief petty officer during World War II)—actually runs everything.

I could go on about the *TR* and its crew at epic length. And one day, if they'll invite me back, I'll do so. But, being a reporter, I wasn't there to report on things. I was there to get a journalistic hook—a tailhook, as it were—for a preconceived idea. I wanted to say something about presidential candidate Senator John McCain. And as soon as our distinguished visitors group donned "float coats" and ear protection and went to the flight deck and saw F-18s take off and land, I had something to say.

Carrier launches are astonishing events. The plane is moved to within what seems like a bowling alley's length of the bow. A blast shield larger than any government building driveway Khomeini-flipper rises behind the fighter jet, and the jet's twin engines are cranked to maximum thrust. A slot-car slot runs down the middle of the bowling alley. The powered-up jet is held at the end of its slot by a steel shear pin smaller than a V8 can. When the shear pin shears, the jet is unleashed and so is a steam catapult that hurls the plane down the slot, from 0 to 130 miles per hour in two seconds. And—if all goes well—the airplane is airborne. This is not a pilot taking off. This is a pilot as cat's-eye marble pinched between boundless thumb and infinite forefinger of Heaven's own Wham-O slingshot.

Carrier landings are more astonishing. We were in heavy seas. Spray was coming over the bow onto the flight deck, sixty feet above the waterline. As the ship was pitching, eighteen tons of F-18 with a wingspan of forty-odd feet approached at the speed of a celebrity sex-assault rumor. Four acres of flight deck have never looked so small. Had it been lawn you'd swear you could do it in fifteen minutes with a push mower.

Four arresting cables are stretched across the stern, each thick as a pepperoni. The cables are held slightly above the runway by metal hoops. The pilot can't really see these cables and isn't really looking at that runway, which is rising at him like a slap in the face or falling away like the slope of a playground slide when you're four. The pilot has his eye on the "meatball," a device, portside midship, with a glowing dot that does—or doesn't—line up between two lighted dashes. This indicates that the pilot is . . . no, isn't . . . yes, is . . . isn't . . . is . . . on course to land. Meanwhile there are sailors in charge of the landing, hunched at a control panel portside aft. They are on the radio telling the pilot what he's doing or better had do or hadn't better. They are also waving colored paddles at him, meaning this or that. (I don't pretend to know what I'm going on about here.) Plus there are other pilots on the radio along with an officer in the control tower. The pilot is very well trained, because at this point his head doesn't explode.

The pilot drops his tailhook. This is not an impressive-looking piece of equipment—no smirks about the 1991 Tailhook Association brouhaha, please. The hook doesn't appear sturdy enough to yank Al Franken offstage when Al is smirking about the presidential candidate who belonged to the Tailhook Association. The hook is supposed to—and somehow usually does—strike the deck between the second and third arresting cables. The cable then does not jerk the F-18 back to the stern the way it would in a cartoon, although watching these events is so unreal that you expect cartoon logic to apply.

Now imagine all concerned doing all of the above with their eyes closed. That is a night operation. We went back on deck to see—wrong verb—to feel and hear the night flights. The only things we could see were the flaming twin suns of the F-18 afterburners at the end of the catapult slot.

Some say John McCain's character was formed in a North Vietnamese prison. I say those people should take a gander at what John chose to do—voluntarily. Being a carrier pilot requires aptitude, intelligence, skill, knowledge, discernment, and courage of a kind rarely found anywhere but in a poem of Homer's or a half-gallon of Dewar's. I look from John McCain to what the opposition has to offer. There's Ms. Smarty-Pantsuit, the Bosnia-under-sniper-fire poster gal, former prominent Washington hostess, and now the JV senator from the state that brought you Eliot Spitzer and Bear Stearns. And there's the happy-talk boy wonder, the plaster Balthazar in the Cook County political crèche, whose policy pronouncements sound like a walk through Greenwich Village in 1968, "Change, man? Got any spare change? Change?"

Some people say John McCain isn't conservative enough. But there's more to conservatism than low taxes, Jesus, and waterboarding at Gitmo. Conservatism is also a matter of honor, duty, valor, patriotism, self-discipline, responsibility, good order, respect for our national institutions, reverence for the traditions of civilization, and adherence to the political honesty upon which all principles of democracy are based. Given what screwups we humans are in these respects, conservatism is also a matter of sense of humor. Heard any good quips lately from Hillary or Barack?

A one-day visit to an aircraft carrier is a lifelong lesson in conservatism. The ship is immense, going seven decks down from the flight deck and ten levels up in the tower. But it's full, with some 5,500 people aboard. Living space is as cramped as steerage on the way to Ellis Island. Even the pilots live in three-bunk cabins as small and windowless as a hall closet. A warship is a sort of giant Sherman tank upon the water. Once belowdecks you're sealed inside. There are no cheery portholes to wave from.

McCain could hardly escape understanding the limits of something huge but hermetic, like a government, and packed with a madding crowd. It requires organization, needs hierarchies, demands meritocracy, insists upon delegation of authority. An intricate, time-tested system replete with checks and balances is not a plaything to be moved around in a dollhouse of ideology. It is not a toy bunny serving imaginary sweets in a make-believe political dollhouse. The captain commands, but his whims do not. He answers to the nation.

And yet an aircraft carrier is more an example of what people can do than what government can't. Scores of people are all over the flight deck during takeoffs and landings. They wear color-coded T-shirts—yellow for flight-directing, purple for fueling, blue for chocking and tying down, red for weapon-loading, brown for I-know-not-what, and so on. These people can't hear each other. They use hand signals. And, come night ops, they can't do that. Really, they communicate by "training telepathy." They have absorbed their responsibilities to the point that each knows exactly where to be and when and doing what.

These are supremely dangerous jobs. And most of the flight deck crew members are only nineteen or twenty. Indeed the whole ship is run by youngsters. The average age, officers and all, is about twenty-four. "These are the same kids," a chief petty officer said, "who, back on land, have their hats bumped to one side and their pants around their knees, hanging out on corners. And here they're in charge of thirty-five-million-dollar airplanes."

The crew is in more danger than the pilots. If an arresting cable breaks—and they do—half a dozen young men and women could be sliced in half. When a plane crashes, a weapon malfunctions, or a fire breaks out, there's no ejection seat for the flight deck crew. While we were on the *Theodore Roosevelt,* a memorial service was held for a crew member who had been swept overboard. Would there have been an admiral and a captain of an aircraft carrier and hundreds of the bravest Americans at a memorial service for you when you were twenty?

Supposedly the "youth vote" is all for Obama. But it's John McCain who actually has put his life in the hands of adolescents on a carrier deck. Supposedly the "women's vote" is . . . well, let's not go too far with this. I can speak to John's honor, duty, valor, patriotism, etc., but I'm not sure how well his self-discipline would have fared if he'd been on an aircraft carrier with more than five hundred beautiful women sailors the way I was. At least John likes women, which is more than we can say about Hillary's attitude toward, for instance, the women in Bill's life, who may constitute nearly a majority of the "women's vote."

These would be interesting subjects to discuss with the *Theodore Roosevelt* shipmates, but time was up.

Back on the COD you're buckled in and told to brace as if for a crash. Whereupon there is a crash. The catapult sends you squashed against your flight harness. And just when you think that everything inside your body is going to blow out your nose and navel, it's over. You're in steady, level flight.

A strange flight it is—from the hard-and-fast reality of a floating island to the fantasy world of American solid ground. In this never-never land a couple of tinhorn Second City shysters—who, put together, don't have the life experience of the lowest-ranking gob-with-a-swab cleaning a head on the Big Stick—presume to run for president of the United States. They're not just running against the hero John Mc-Cain; they're running against heroism itself and against almost everything about America that ought to be conserved.

And a few months later John McCain chose Sarah Palin as his vice presidential running mate, and . . . Oh, never mind.

14

White Man Speak with Forked Tongue
The Field Museum, Chicago, May 2008

❖

The Field Museum of Natural History in Chicago has a new permanent exhibit of savagery and barbarism, "The Ancient Americans." The ancient Americans themselves are not portrayed as savage or barbarous. (*How* surprising. Knock me over with a *feather*.) The savages and barbarians are the museum's curators. They plunder history, ravage archaeology, do violence to intelligence, and lay waste to wisdom, faith, and common sense.

At the Field Museum the bygone aboriginal inhabitants of our hemisphere are shown to be regular folks, the same as you and me, although usually more naked and always more noble. Ancient Americans have attained the honored, illustrious status of chumps and fall guys. Never mind that

they were here for 12,000 or 13,000 years before the rest
of us showed up with our pistols and pox, so most of their
getting shafted was, perforce, a do-it-yourself thing.

And also never mind that "The Ancient Americans" exhibit tells you nothing a fourth-grader doesn't know. I am
the parent of a fourth-grader. I live in a house cluttered
with twig and Play-Doh models of hogans, longhouses, and
wickiups, hung with ill-made dream catchers, and strewn
with poorly glued miniature birch bark canoes shedding
birch bark on the rugs. My daughter Muffin's bedroom is
heaped with the apparel, equipage, and chattel of Kaya, the
Native American American Girl doll. The bookshelves in
the fourth-grade classroom overflow with culturally sensitive
and ecologically aware retellings of Potawatomi, Paiute, and
Kickapoo legends, colorfully illustrated by women who use
birds or mammals for their last names.

When I was in fourth grade, some fifty years ago, my
grandmother would take me to the Field Museum. It was a
solemn, quiet, awe-engendering place. All of creation's won-
ders were on display in orderly ranks. Dim corridors were
lined with dioramas featuring important animals—shot,
stuffed, and carefully labeled. Further corridors held won-
ders of a sterner kind: sinister masks from Africa, demon
deities of the heathen Raj, alarming Sung dynasty figurines
depicting the exquisite tortures of Chinese hell. Whatever
steadiness of nerve I now possess I owe to steeling myself
to walk past the display case containing an unwrapped
Egyptian mummy.

The Field Museum was interesting even in its least in-
teresting parts. The section devoted to "Useful Varieties of
Wood" fascinated me in the exactitude of its tediousness.
The world was full of things and—if I could summon the

patience and concentration—those things could be organized, understood, and made to serve a purpose.

The museum fueled every worthy ambition. The min-
eralogical collection made me decide to become a man of
learning and means sufficient to lead an expedition to find
an immense amethyst geode, which I would present to Jennifer Riley, she of the auburn hair in my fourth-grade class,
one row over and two desks up. And the large, gloomy hall
devoted to life in the Arctic was a religious inspiration.
I looked at the full-scale cutaway of winter quarters in
Mackenzie Bay, where you lived in an underground room
the size of a Buick, wore itchy sealskins, ate raw whale,
and breathed the smoke of a caribou chip fire. I would
bow my head and intone, "Praise God for not making me
an Eskimo."

Then Grandmother and I would go to lunch in the
museum's cafeteria, an austere room that served school food
of the better kind—much as the White House Mess does
to this day. Over this comforting fare I would quiz my own
family's ancient American.

"Grandma, what's the difference between Democrats and
Republicans?"

"Democrats rent."

"Grandma, what's wrong with the people in the bad
neighborhoods that we saw from the el?"

"No one is ever so poor that he can't pick up his yard."

"Grandma, which Roosevelt was worse, Teddy or
Franklin?"

"Theodore. He had no business meddling in things the
way he did after your great-grandfather's friend Mr. McKin-
ley died, and he divided the Republican Party, allowing that
scallywag Woodrow Wilson to become the president."

One of the best pleasures of my childhood was to walk hand in hand with my grandmother up the broad flights of marble steps to the towering bronze doors of the Field Museum. The doors are closed now. The main entrance to the museum is no longer used. These days that neoclassical portico with its view of Loop, lakefront, and Grant Park grandeur probably makes people feel small. The back door has more room for tour buses and handicapped ramps. Grandeur is out of style anyway. The Field Museum was built for Chicago's Columbian Exposition of 1892, celebrating (if you can imagine celebrating such a thing) Columbus's "discovery" of America. It wasn't the happiest 400th anniversary for ancient Americans.

The museum is full of noisy children and their caregivers, blended families, and whatever else we're calling kith and kin these days. A long, mouse-maze, airport security–style line must be endured to get tickets. The sculpture of a Masai spearman facing off against a crouching lioness has been shunted to a lonely corner, lest someone somehow take offense. Nowadays offense is taken—snatched and grabbed—as if offense were something valuable to own. And, given our umbrage-fueled national politics, maybe it is. The brontosaurus has been pushed to the back (that is to say the front) of the main hall and isn't called a brontosaurus anymore. (Doubtless offense was taken by Chicago's Bronto-American community.) Nor is the skeleton of this vast vegan any longer engaged in postmortem mortal combat with the bones of a Tyrannosaurus rex. Modern kids are too loving and caring about dinosaurs to be exposed to such scenes of domestic violence.

Most of the minerals and all of the useful woods have been replaced by a gift shop the size of Macy's (appropriately enough, since Macy's is now the name on Marshall Field's, department store, whose founder was the Field Museum's patron). The cafeteria is gone; McDonald's has been installed. At least people are still dressed the way I was half a century ago: in jeans or shorts, T-shirts, and gym shoes. Except that these are people of forty or fifty. Indeed, some are as old as my grandmother was when she, in hat and gloves, escorted me. And Grandma had first visited the Field Museum during the Columbian exposition.

I couldn't see what the children are wearing; they are misbehaving blurs to my bifocaled eyes. None seems afraid to walk past the mummy case. I didn't have the heart. Unwrapped as he is, with aged body parts on view, the mummy fits in too well, sartorially, with a twenty-first-century crowd.

At the portal of "The Ancient Americans" exhibit is the first of many, many wall inscriptions telling you what you should be thinking, if you happen to do any of that.

> The Ancient Americans is a story of diversity and change— not progress.

Were this a criticism of pre-Columbian societies, you'd be in for an interesting experience. It isn't. You aren't.

Besides the wall inscriptions, the exhibit is cluttered with innumerable video screens displaying people yakking in native languages described as nearly extinct. What information is conveyed thereby, and to whom, is an open question.

An extensive collection of Inca clay faces appears opposite the "not progress" message. The Incas seem to have been skilled cartoonists in the Wallace and Gromit manner. However, Claymation lacks something when it isn't animated. But that's not-progress for you.

"Gallery guides available in Spanish only," reads another wall inscription. This is either overdoing it with multiculturalism or an implied insult to the effect that Hispanics are too stupid to find their way through an exhibit arranged like a drunkard's version of the museum's ticket line.

A very wordy inscription details the theories of when and how humans arrived in the New World. Translated from the Academese: "We dunno." An encomium to the Ice Age hunter-gatherers follows. "People like us," it concludes, "prospered in ancient times." We did indeed—if your idea of prosperity is fastening a "Clovis people" spear point to a stick and stabbing long-horned bison, giant ground sloths, woolly mammoths, mastodons, and New World horses until they were all extinct. The economic boom didn't extend to casual wear and sports clothes. Ice Age or no, everyone in the talentlessly painted murals is naked. Nipples seem to have been vague and smudgy in ancient times, and a mastodon or giant ground sloth was always getting in between mural viewers and your genitals.

Under one such painting a caption reads:

> "Look at that mammoth," your aunt cries out as you hike downhill toward a vast plain. "The men [sic!] did well . . . " Your family and other group members pause to give thanks and honor the mammoth whose life was taken. . . .

The Americas were peopled, presciently, by future Californians.

"After the Ice Age," reads another wall, "human creativity made the Americas more culturally diverse." Barack Obama was elected, I guess.

Nearby is a large mural titled "Eastern Woodlands 2500 BC–500 BC." I'm a resident of the Eastern Woodlands and, except for fewer naked people, they haven't changed much.

Perhaps the title should be amended to "Eastern Woodlands 2500 BC–500 BC and in AD 1969 When Janis Joplin and Santana Were Performing at Woodstock." The naked people in the Eastern Woodlands "faced growing population and environmental stresses. This led to periods of conflict with their neighbors." Fortunately, Chief Obama was willing, without diplomatic preconditions, to meet and negotiate with any ancient American leader. Therefore the "periods of conflict" didn't result in anything like, oh, members of the Iroquois confederation capturing, torturing, enslaving, and occasionally eating everyone they could get their hands on.

An office cubicle's space is allotted to the Mound Builders. Who were they? Why did they build the mounds? How did they do it? Was there free parking? Translating, again, from the Academese: "Got me, pal."

Then comes a prolix wall headed "Powerful Leaders."

> Why did people give up power to make some of their own decisions? Central decision makers were often more effective than groups at organizing large amounts of labor, managing resources, and directing wars.

So maybe it was Hillary, not Obama, who got elected. This brings us to the Maya and their abominable customs, nicely glossed:

> . . . Sacrifice has played a role in the religious beliefs of many people throughout history and in all parts of the world. . . . Even today almost all world religions include sacrifice of some kind in their spiritual practices.

Now wait a damn minute, you infidel apes of social science. Shut your Brie holes and listen up. God, *the* God, the God who didn't make me an Eskimo, does not require human sacrifice; he *suffers* it. "For God so loved the world, that he gave his only begotten Son, that whosoever believeth in him should not perish, but have everlasting life." That is the difference—perhaps the only difference—between civilization and savagery. And it's not just we Christians who say so. From the time of Abraham no monotheist has practiced human sacrifice; no Buddhist ever has, and no Hindu since the days of suttee and the Thugs. No Taoist, no Confucian, no Zoroastrian, Bahaist, or Sikh includes murder in his "spiritual practices."

The text on the Maya continues:

> Some societies in the ancient Americas, like the Maya, practiced bloodletting or human sacrifice as part of their ceremonies or spiritual beliefs. Why? Anthropologists don't fully know.

Let's finish that sentence. "Anthropologists don't fully know *the difference between right and wrong.*"

In a nook around the corner from "Mayan Spirituality" a computer-animated movie runs on a continuous loop. "Living in a State Society" offers a different definition of civilization. "State Societies" are, it seems, all societies in which sticks and grass aren't the principal constituents of housing, wardrobe, and diet. The movie explains that, in a State Society, the "Ruling Classes" are supported by the "State Power Triad" consisting of the Economy, the Military, and Religion. "For the first time," the narrator drones, "the ruling class had a different standard of living than others. Why would people want to give up their freedom? For most there was no choice."

The message of the movie is, I think, to build a wig-
wam, wear a hula skirt, and boil some sticks for dinner. Or
maybe the message is to pack the car and move to North
Korea. Or, possibly, the message is to get over it, accept Big
Chief Obama or Big Chief Hillary, as the case may be, and
learn to love his or her tax hikes, retreat from promoting
international democracy, and practice Mayan-style spiritual
beliefs (including health care bloodletting) because "there
was no choice."

After a twist and a turn in the exhibit's vagrant route
you are among the Aztecs and Incas. The loathsome Aztecs
devoted most of their energy to human sacrifices, horrifying
in extent and gruesome in technique. "The Ancient Americans" treats this in a moving-right-along manner.

> From mild bloodletting to violent death, sacrifice offered
> thanks to the gods while maintaining the natural order of
> the world.

The original "New World Order," as it were. Inscriptions also
give a nod to media hype:

> The Spanish often emphasized accounts of bloodthirsty sac-
> rifice to justify conquering the Aztec people.

You're hustled past the Incas' no doubt better-justified
conquerings. You enter a hushed and funereal room with
tombstone lettering on black walls.

> WHEN WORLDS COLLIDE
> In 1492, the first European explorers arrived in the Americas,
> triggering a devastating loss of life almost inconceivable to
> us today.

Joseph Stalin, please go to the white courtesy phone. The wall inscription proceeds:

> Here, we reflect on the magnitude of loss inflicted on America's Indigenous peoples by European invasion.

The European inflictions are grimly illustrated. The first one upon which we are expected to reflect is the only decent thing (not counting the wheel, iron, cigarette papers, etc.) that Europeans brought to America's Indigenous peoples, "Religious Conversion." Second is "Disease," which should stir our sympathy but hardly our guilt. The exhibit points out that disease was the chief cause of suffering after European contact. Therefore, the horrors that beset "The Ancient Americans" following 1492 would have happened if the *Niña,* the *Pinta,* and the *Santa María* had been manned by Jimmy Carter, the Dalai Lama, and Bono.

You escape the pity parlor of "When Worlds Collide" and traverse a space of video screen talking heads and interactive displays with all their buttons being pounded by toddlers. This is "Living Descendants." The ancient Americans' modern relations are regular folks, as their ancestors were, and with clothes on, too, the same as you and me. Of course, if they're the same as you and me, why do they need a room in a museum any more than we do? Well, "despite centuries of injustice and oppression, today's Indigenous peoples strive to sustain their cultural traditions."

You could say the same of the Irish. Being one, I looked for the exit to go find a drink. I wandered into a solemn, quiet, awe-engendering place. The large, gloomy hall devoted to life in the Arctic was now incorporated into "The Ancient Americans." I saw, once again, the full-scale cutaway of Eskimo winter quarters in Mackenzie Bay. Its labels are curled and yellowing but unchanged—respectful, factual, precise. The ancient Americans weren't regular folks. They lived strange, spectacular lives on strange, spectacular continents heretofore untrod by man and more remote for them than Mars—or the world of museum curation—is for us. The ancient Americans were tough as hell. They did their share of nasty stuff. But even the Aztecs don't deserve to be patronized, demeaned, and insulted by what is—or is supposed to be, or once was—one of the white man's great institutions of learning.

Give "The Ancient Americans" exhibit back to the ancient Americans, and the Field Museum along with it. If any of the heirs and assignees of the Aztecs, Incas, or Maya feel inclined to practice a little human sacrifice on anthropologists, sociologists, moral relativists, neo-Marxists, and other conquistadors of modern academia, call it "maintaining the natural order of the world."

15

The Decline and Fall of Tomorrow

Disneyland, June 2008

❖

More than half a century ago, Disneyland opened its "House of the Future" attraction. I was ten, and I was attracted. In fact, I was in love.

The Tomorrowland dwelling had a cruciform floor plan, a more elegant solution to bringing light and air into a "machine for living" than Le Corbusier had been able to devise. Each side of each arm of the X was glazed, sill to ceiling. The mullions and rails between the panes were as pleasingly orchestrated as Mondrian's black stripes. All the proportions of the home (and a home was what I saw in this house) were pleasing. Proportions are when they match the "Golden Rectangle." The human eye loves a ratio of .618034 to 1 or, roughly, 5 by 8. Both Pythagoras and Euclid called it the

"Divine Section." It's the mathematical value that generates the shape of the galaxies, the Fibonacci sequence, the spiral of seashells, the Parthenon's configuration, and a little piece of Disneyland circa 1957.

Of course, at ten, my critique of the House of the Future was, "It's neat." But, within the limits of childish understanding, I would have tried to explain. I was an architecture fan the way my friends were sports fans. I was a Frank Lloyd Wright Prairie School booster. But I had a soft spot for the neoclassical, even though, as a member of the modernist pep club, I knew I wasn't supposed to. (Just as there were certain kids who had nursed a secret hope that the Yankees would beat the Brooklyn Dodgers in the 1956 World Series.) And I couldn't help booing the diluted, piddle-colored brick version of the International Style that filled the construction sites of my childhood. The only way you could tell a shopping center from a grade school from a minimum-security prison was by the amount of flood-lighting and fence wire involved.

Disney's House of the Future had the clean simplicity prized in the 1950s as relief from decades of frayed patchwork, jury-rigging, and make-do clutter caused by Depression and war. But the HoF wasn't marred by starkness. The spare white form had been warmed with curves. Each quadrant was a streamlined seamed pod, a crossbreed: half jet fuselage, half legume. And, as with an airplane or a beanstalk, the structure rose aloft, flying on a plinth above its house lot.

This was not the domicile's most practical feature when it came to helping Mom unload the groceries from the DeSoto Fireflite station wagon. (Chrysler Corporation's advertising slogan in 1957: "Suddenly it's 1960!") But levitation sure would have enlarged my weenie subdivision yard. There'd be room for a bit of Tomorrowland for my own family, or, anyway, a trampoline. I remember wondering what our "colonial" (which didn't even merit the prefix pseudo-) would look like jacked up eight feet and plopped on a shaft. Better, definitely.

The House of the Future was sponsored by the Monsanto Company and designed by Marvin Goody and Richard Hamilton from the MIT architecture department. They were prescient in various unimportant ways: the residence contained cordless phones, a flat-screen, wall-size TV; and a somewhat sinister-sounding device called a "microwave oven." Otherwise the only relationship between the futurism and the future was that today, in Los Angeles and New York, every bit of the place would be worth tens of thousands of dollars as a precious "Mid-Century Modern" antique.

The most nostalgically futuristic aspect of the House of the Future was that it was made almost entirely of plastic. In 1957 plastic still enjoyed the benefit of its definition (2a) in Merriam-Webster's: "capable of being molded and shaped"—into anything you wanted! Plastic was the stuff that didn't rust or rot or break when you dropped it. Thanks to plastic and a little glue, even the clumsiest kid (me) could build splendidly detailed models of PanAm Mars Passenger Rockets and atomic-powered automobiles and all the other things that wouldn't happen. We were a decade away from the scene in *The Graduate* that made the word an epithet. I, for one, think Dustin Hoffman's character should have taken the career advice, and the stupid movie should have ended then and there. Instead, in 1967, it was Disney's House of the Future that came to an abrupt finish. Or not-so-abrupt. Reports have it that a wrecking ball merely bounced on the sturdy polymer seed cases, and the prematurely postmodernist structure had to be sawed apart by hand. (As many a timorous would-be suicide has discovered—with vise-like grip on a bridge railing—the future is harder to get rid of than you'd think.)

Tomorrowland survived being homeless. But it lost its zest. Walt had died in 1966, and Disney Inc. was deprived of his instinct for America's flights of fancy. For example, Tomorrowland's Hall of Chemistry closed that same year, just as an entire generation of me and my friends got *very* interested in chemicals.

Nothing speaks of living in the present like getting a complete makeover, which Tomorrowland endured in 1998. Disney, displaying one of the greatest absences of irony on record, gave Tomorrowland a "retro" theme.

Disney's press release called the new Tomorrowland "a classic future environment." This explains the Astro Orbiter ride, built in a style that might be called "Jules Vernacular," with lots of exposed rivet heads, ogee-shaped pieces of wrought iron containing circular holes, and rockets with nose cones like the Eiffel Tower. "Classic future" also excuses the Chevron-sponsored Autopia, a holdover from the Tomorrowland of yore where tourists can drive on a "superhighway"—with divided lanes!—in quarter-scale fiberglass imitations of the dream cars at auto shows when Ike was in office.

My family and I arrived at Disneyland on a hot June day. We had spent the preceding two hours stuck in traffic on an un-super Interstate 5, idling away $4.35 gasoline in a rental car that was no one's idea of a dream. Autopia did not appeal.

But there was a part of moldy old Tomorrowland that wasn't past its sell-by date. A fresh-minted House of the Future had had its ribbon-cutting—with laser scissors?—earlier that month. These digs were completely original and all brand (specifically: Microsoft, Hewlett-Packard and Life|ware brand) new.

Mrs. O. took our younger children, Poppet and Buster, "to infinity and beyond" (Buzz Lightyear being integral to the classic future's canon). And I led ten-year-old Muffin to utopia's latest abode.

Muffin, like her dad as a kid, is a midget aesthete, though with an interest more in interior than edifice. She has a good eye (if somewhat too great a fondness for cute kittens). My wife and I actually consult her about paint colors and where pictures should be hung. I didn't tell Muffin what I was up to, or Disney's press office, either. We eschewed friendly hovering. I wanted my daughter's gut reaction. And if that gut reaction was as strong and as positive as mine had been in 1957, if Muffin uttered the 2008 kidspeak translation of "It's neat"— "Omigod, awesome"—then we, as a civilization, are doomed.

I say this because I'd read a February 13 Associated Press story by Gillian Flaccus, "Disney Rebuilds 'House of the Future' with Tech Giants' Help." Various passages caught my attention and piqued my blood pressure: "Lights and thermostats will automatically adjust when people walk into a room." My wife, for example. All winter long—with heating oil costing more per gallon than the brand of vodka we've been reduced to buying—my wife walks into a room, and the thermostat is adjusted to eighty degrees. First that sentence from the AP started a fight in my mind with my wife. Then the next sentence turned my wife on me, tooth and nail: "Closets will help pick out the right dress for a party." The article went on to explain, "Mirrors and closets could identify clothes and suggest matching outfits." Imagine having a full-length looking glass *and* a husband tell you, "That makes your butt look big."

Following upon the stifling bedroom with its closet full of body image insecurities and bitchy fashion comments came, "Countertops will be able to identify groceries set on them and make menu suggestions." You've just come back from a family trip to the Shop-N-Pay. (And, I gather, in the new House of the Future, you don't have to beam up the canned goods from the sub-household carport.) The tantrums over checkout lane candy and gum and the attempts to avert children's eyes from the cover of *Us* are over. Sticker shock has worn off. Everybody's in a pretty good mood. And suddenly the strip of Formica between the sink and the stove pipes up in a computer-generated snivel: "I hate asparagus." "Muffin took all the Skittles." "Meat loaf *again*?" Probably the fridge chimes in, "Well, if you don't like meat loaf make your own damn dinner." And this is assuming that the kitchen doesn't have IT problems or an e-mail virus or an inputting error that causes the countertop to go, "macaroniandcheesemacaroniandcheesemacaroniand . . ." We already have a four-year-old who does that.

"Much of the project," Flaccus wrote, "will showcase a network that makes the house 'smart' and follows family members from room to room—even adjusting artwork—to preset personal preferences."

So I enter the "great room." (HoF II is described as having 5,000 square feet and only two bedrooms, so I assume we've got a McMansion here.) I encounter bracing fresh air, Remington bronzes, and Buddy Holly on the sound system. My wife is greeted with cozy warmth, abstract expressionism, and Bach. Muffin receives kitten portraits and the *High School Musical* score. Her younger siblings, Poppet and Buster, get plush toys, Tonka trucks, and Raffi tunes.

But what happens when we all walk in together? Just how smart is this house? Does it launch into a pathetic attempt to make everybody happy? Norman Rockwell limned some kittens and a cowboy or two and even an illustration of a museum guard puzzling over a Jackson Pollock. Maybe the Boston Pops does "Baby Beluga" to a rockabilly beat. There could be a blazing fire on one side and a freezing draft on the other. Or does the smart house, like many brainy types, get angry when it's conflicted? Our living space turns into a sauna hung with hellish works of Francis Bacon while Philip Glass blares and all the playthings come from China slathered in lead paint. I showed the AP article to my wife. She said, "You don't sell a house like this; you divorce it."

Muffin and I trudged across Tomorrowland, following intermittent and unenthusiastic signage, toward the House of the Future. The way in was at the top of a spiral ramp that should have been an Archimedes' screw of a people mover, or something, especially since it ascended a building that once held the "General Electric Carousel of Progress." (This merry-go-round of human improvement broke down in 1973.) Muffin asked where we were going. I told her and she said, "So it's really, really, modern?" It was more modern than that. HoF II has a subprime mortgage, or so it appeared. The joint was closed up.

"Technical difficulties," said a Disney "cast member."

I listened at the roped-off entrance for a telltale sound of "macaroniandcheesemacaroniandcheesemacaroniandcheese," but I heard nothing. So one had to wonder.

I invoked what media privileges I have and called Disney public relations. John McClintock, a senior publicist, could not have been more polite and understanding. He did what he could to get my daughter and me just a walk-through and a look-around. That was all you got with the old House of the Future anyway, although HoF II comes with performers portraying a future family (which still has one mom and one dad, amazingly enough). I understand you'll get to visit with them while they play-act packing for a trip to China—posters of Chairman Mao on the "adjusting art"; tunes from *Flower Drum Song* playing in the background; closets scolding, "That will get *so* wrinkled in the suitcase"; and countertop warning, "Don't order snake."

McClintock called back. "Technical difficulties," he said, plus a firm no-go from his higher-ups.

Muffin and I could look over a railing into the ceiling-free household one floor below us. It has a single-story open plan with a circular shape, though the circularity seems to have more to do with the roundness of the old Carousel of Progress and crowd control than with futurism. Not that there were any crowds trying to get in. As far as I could tell nobody but Muffin and I noticed that HoF II wasn't open.

I boosted Muffin so she could get a better view. Her preteen snarkiness blended with childish disappointment. "It looks like our hotel," she said.

Not even. And where we were staying was best described as "Schlitz-Carlton."

According to Disney, the shape of things to come takes shape at Pottery Barn, with a quick stop in Restoration Hardware for "classic future" touches and a trip to Target to get throw rugs and cheap Japanese paper lanterns. HoF II was designed by the Taylor Morrison company, a home builder specializing in anodyne subdevelopmental housing in the Southwest. The company's president and CEO told the Associated Press, "The 1950s home didn't look like anything, anywhere. It was space-age and kind of cold. We didn't want the home to intimidate the visitors."

Muffin wasn't scared. To my profound relief she wasn't interested at all. Though, in fairness, only a few of the HoF II innovations were discernible from our perch. The art on the walls, set in fussy gilt frames, did keep changing. I couldn't see quite what the changes were, but I'm guessing Manet to Monet and back.

The variegating artwork summoned memories of my Great-Aunt Lillian's annual visits. She was a very amateur painter. On the day before her arrival my mother would make a frantic rush to the attic to dig out her wealthy, childless relative's oeuvre. (Many depictions of kittens, as I recall.) Unfaded spaces on our wallpaper did not match the shapes of Aunt Lil's paintings, and she left us nothing in her will.

A coffee table in HoF II displayed, via Power Point–type projection, the text and original John Tenniel illustrations of *Alice in Wonderland*. "Daddy, read me a coffee table." Family photos were scattered around, cased in conventional silver plate. But there was something lap-toppy about the backs of the pictures that suggested they were video capable. Uncle Mike on the mantel, forever recounting his Iwo Jima exploits.

HoF II's kitchen table had plasma screen place mats showing water rippling over rocks—just the sort of thing a drinking man wants waving away under his eggs in the morning.

I asked Muffin, "Well, what do you think of the House of the Future?"

"It's beige," she said. Beige it is, literally—upholstered, carpeted, and painted in brownish, grayish, yellowish hues. And beige it is metaphorically. Any random dull normal person (we have one in our house) could come up with snappier ideas for the future than HoF II seems to contain. How about self-washing windows? Automobiles have had them since the 1930s. And have you watched the clever manner by which modern convertible car tops operate? What keeps that technology from being applied to self-making beds? If a house *must* be smart (and, as a man who is continually outwitted by his wife, children, and dogs, the house can dummy up and mind its own beeswax as far as I'm concerned), then why can't it be as smart as a Toyota? Toyotas start their wipers at the first drop of rain. I wouldn't mind a house that could close its own windows, although I'm sure my thumb will be there when they slam shut.

Such ideas are too simply reasonable for Tomorrowland. In HoF II, according to the AP, "When a resident clicks a TV remote . . . lights will dim, music will shut off and the shades will draw. . . ." What if it's a beautiful day outside, I'm reading the paper and humming along to "Hello Peggy Sue," and I just want to check the NASDAQ?

I saw no mention of the Disney house having one of those robot vacuum cleaners that trundles around hoovering on its own agenda. I hope HoF II at least has that. I want to see it face off against my Boston bull terrier. I'm giving two-to-one odds against the vacuum. Even better would be a helium balloon with a propeller and a mop of feathers that flew around dusting things. It might not do a very good job dusting, but at our house, neither do we.

I polled the family, to get their ideas of how a domicile could be inventive. My wife suggested that the "smart" closet cut the wisecracks about her knockoff Jimmy Choos and close its doors and do the dry cleaning (with ecologically friendly solvents, of course). She also proposed a "face bidet" for chocolate-smeared kiddies and an iPod "nag chip" that periodically interrupts to tell children to do their homework, clean their rooms, etc.

Muffin wants to install hot air dryers in our shower "to save the earth's towels." She also has an idea for a spiral slide from her bedroom to the garage. The chute would be rigged with her clothes so that she could slide right into them. Homework and packed lunch would be pressed into her hands and milk, juice, and cereal piped into her mouth as she descended to the backseat of the car. Thus Muffin figures she could go from bed to being on the way to school in one minute flat.

Poppet, our eight-year-old, envisions a system of pneumatic tubes that would deliver the stuffed animal of her choosing to the place of her choice, worldwide.

Buster, who's four, said, "Dogs on the potty." A serious challenge to the plumbing industry, not to mention the dogs, but it's a worthy goal.

Even if Microsoft, Hewlett-Packard, and Life|ware have no ideas whatsoever you'd think they could tap Disney's proven reserves of whimsy. Where's Mrs. Teapot, her son Chip, the officious candlestick, and the chairs that walk around in *Beauty and the Beast*? Where is the *plastic* inventiveness of Mickey and Donald cartoons? Where is Gyro Gearloose when we need him?

Denigrating the future has been a main prop of the intellectual edifice for the past forty years. Looking forward went out of fashion about the time that Buckminster Fuller's audacious geodesic domes, meant to cover entire cities, wound up as hippie-height wobbling commune structures cobbled together out of barn boards. Bruce Handy, writing in *Time* about Disney's 1998 reopening of a deliberately out-of-date Tomorrowland, began his essay with the sentence, "The future isn't what it used to be." He stated, "It's not a novel observation to point out that our culture has become increasingly backward looking." And he asked, "Hasn't life become messier as it's become easier?"

Don't blame the future. For one thing, it doesn't exist yet. And, for another thing, we do. We're always creating our future whether we mean to or think so or don't. Global creativity, like global climate, seems to have its cycles—natural, man-made, or whatever. Sometimes human beings just aren't very imaginative. There was our first million years of existence as a species, for starters. We came down from the trees, made some stone choppers, and that was it.

The last thousand years of the Roman Empire, until the fall of Constantinople, were no great shakes. The Romans had all the engineering knowledge needed to start an industrial revolution. But they preferred to have toga parties and let slaves do all the work.

The Chinese had gunpowder, but it didn't occur to them to put it in a gun. They possessed the compass but didn't go anywhere. They invented paper, printing, and a written form of their language, but hardly anyone in China was taught to read.

And here we are now. Name a cherished contemporary avant-garde painter or novelist. Name a great living composer. Say "Andrew Lloyd Webber" and I'll throttle you. Theater is revivals and revivals of revivals and stuff like making a musical out of old Kellogg's Rice Krispies commercials with Nathan Lane as "Snap." Movies are famously not any good anymore. More modern poetry is written than read. Modern architecture leaks and the builders left their plumb bobs at home. The most prominent contemporary art form is one that is completely unimaginative (or is supposed to be), the memoir. To top it all, we have just experienced perhaps the greatest technological advance in the history of mankind. And what are we using the Internet for? To sell each other eight-track tapes on eBay, tell complete strangers the location of all our tattoos on Facebook, and, if Tomorrowland is anything to go by, turn our houses into nattering, shrieking, dysfunctional reality TV shows even when nobody's home.

I took a last look into the homestead of the hereafter and said to Muffin, "Let's get out of here."

She was nothing loath. I asked, "What do *you* think will happen in the future?"

"You'll buy me a humongous ice cream cone."

16

A JOURNEY TO . . . LET'S NOT GO THERE
Summer 2008

❖

Part 1

I looked death in the face. All right, I didn't. I glimpsed him in a crowd. I was diagnosed with cancer, of a very treatable kind. I'm told I have a 95 percent chance of survival. Come to think of it—as a drinking, smoking, saturated-fat-hound of a reporter—my chance of survival has been improved by cancer.

I still cursed God, as we all do when we get bad news and pain. Not even the most faith-impaired among us shouts, "Damn quantum mechanics!" "Damn organic chemistry!" "Damn chaos and coincidence!"

I believe in God. God created the world. Obviously pain had to be included in God's plan. Otherwise we'd never learn that our actions have consequences. Our cave-dwelling ancestors, finding fire warm, would conclude that curling up to sleep in the middle of the flames would be even warmer. Cave bears would dine on roast ancestor, and we'd never experience any pain because we wouldn't be here.

But God, Sir, in Your manner of teaching us about life's consequential nature, isn't death a bit . . . um . . . extreme, pedagogically speaking? I know the lesson that we're studying is difficult. But dying is a harder final exam than I was counting on. Also, it kind of messes up my vacation planning. Can we talk after class? Maybe if I did something for extra credit . . .

Seeing things from God's point of view is difficult for a mortal. The more so for a mortal who's just received an updated mortality scheduling memo from the pathology department.

Seeing things from God's point of view is the purpose of conventional religion, in my opinion. And I am a conventionally religious person. But I feel the need to think through a few things before I unload my gripes on Father Hoolihan. He's got a busy parish and he isn't as young as he used to be. In fact Father Hoolihan doesn't look well himself. Perhaps, if I can get my thoughts straight, he can unload his gripes on me. I can't give him last rites, but I can give him a whiskey.

Why can't death—if we must have it—be always glorious, as in The Iliad? Of course death continues to be so, sometimes, with heroes in Fallujah and Kandahar. But nowadays death more often comes drooling on the toilet seat in the nursing home or bleeding under the crushed roof of a teen-driven SUV or breathless in a deluxe hotel suite filled with empty drug bottles and a minor public figure whose celebrity expiration date has passed. I have, of all the inglorious things, a malignant hemorrhoid. What color bracelet does one wear for that? And where does one wear it? And what slogan is apropos? Perhaps that slogan can be sewn in needlepoint around the ruffle on a cover for my embarrassing little doughnut buttocks pillow.

Furthermore, I am a logical, sensible, pragmatic Republican, and my diagnosis came just weeks after Teddy Kennedy's. That *he* should have cancer of the brain, and *I* should have cancer of the ass . . . Well, I said a rosary for him and hoped he had a laugh at me. After all, what would I do, ask God for a more dignified cancer? Pancreas? Liver? Lung?

Which brings me to the nature of my prayers. They are, like most prayers from most people, abject self-pleadings. But praying for oneself has disturbing implications. There's Saint Teresa's warning about answered prayers or, for our atheistic friends, the tale of "The Monkey's Paw."

And I can't be the only person who feels like a jerk saying, "Please cure me, God. I'm underinsured. I have three little children. And I have three dogs, two of which will miss me. And my wife will cry and mourn and be inconsolable and have to get a job. P.S. Our mortgage is subprime."

God knows this stuff. He's God. He's all-knowing. What am I telling Him, really? "Gosh, You sure are a good God. Good—You own it. Plus, You're infinitely wise, infinitely merciful, but . . . Look, everybody makes mistakes. A little cancer of the behind, it's not a big mistake. Not something that's going on Your personal record. Let's not think of it as a mistake. Let's think of it as a teachable moment. Nobody's so good that He or She can't improve, so . . ."

It's one universe, entire, God's creation and all of a piece. There's a theory about how the fluttering of a butterfly's wing can somehow eventually cause a cyclone in the Bay of

Bengal or something like that. What if the flatulence of me in a radiation therapy session eventually causes . . . I mean, suppose Saint Peter had my fax number and faxed me: "P.J., we did the math. We can get you a 100 percent survival rate instead of 95 percent, but twenty years from now a volcanic eruption in Honduras will kill 700,000 people." What do I fax back? "Dear Saint Peter, Thank God. That's a real shame about Honduras. I promise I'll donate $1,000 to the International Red Cross."

I think I'll pray for fortitude instead and, maybe, for relief from gas.

No doubt death is one of those mysterious ways in which God famously works. Except, upon consideration, death isn't mysterious. Do we really want *everyone* to be around *forever?* I'm thinking about my own family, specifically a certain stepfather I had as a kid. Sayonara, you SOB. On the other hand, Napoleon was doubtless a great man in his time; at least the French think so. But do we want even Napoleon extant in perpetuity? Do we want him always escaping from island exiles, raising fanatically loyal troops of soldiers, invading Russia, and burning Moscow? Well, at the moment, considering Putin et al., maybe we do want that. But, century after century, it would get old. And what with Genghis Khan coming from the other direction all the time and Alexander the Great clashing with a Persia that is developing nuclear weapons and Roman legions destabilizing already precarious Israeli-Palestinian relations—things would be a mess.

Then there's the matter of our debt to death for life as we know it. I believe in God. I also believe in evolution. If death weren't around to "finalize" the Darwinian process, we'd all still be amoebas. We'd eat by surrounding pizzas with our belly flab and have sex by lying on railroad tracks waiting for a train to split us into significant others. I consider evolution to be more than a scientific theory. I think it's a call to God. God created a free universe. He could have created any kind of universe He wanted. But a universe without freedom would have been static and meaningless—a taxpayer-funded-art-in-public-places universe.

Rather, God created a universe full of cosmic whatchamajiggers and subatomic whosits free to interact. And interact they did, becoming matter and organic matter and organic matter that replicated itself and life. And this life was completely free, as amoral as my cancer cells.

Life-forms could exercise freedom to an idiotic extent, growing uncontrolled, thoughtless, and greedy to the point that they killed the source of their own fool existence. But, with the help of death, matter began to learn right from wrong—how to save itself and its ilk, how to nurture, how to love (or, anyway, how to build a Facebook page), and how to know God and His rules.

Death is so important that God visited death upon His own Son, thereby helping us learn right from wrong well enough that we may escape death forever and live eternally in God's grace. (Although this option is not usually open to reporters.)

I'm not promising that the Pope will back me up about all of the above. But it's the best I can do by my poor lights about the subject of mortality and free will. Thus, the next time I glimpse death . . . Well, I'm not going over and introducing myself. I'm not giving the grim reaper fist dabs. But I'll remind myself to try, at least, to thank God for death. And then I'll thank God, with all my heart, for whiskey.

Part 2

A diagnosis of cancer raises deep metaphysical questions such as, "Is God a nice guy?" and "Will my bird dog go to heaven or do I flush the quail of paradise with seraphim, cherubim, and putti?"

But after a while diagnosis wears off. It's time for an intermission in the self-dramatization of "I Have a Life-Threatening Disease." I wasn't able to play the role to its full tragical effect anyway. The kind of cancer I had was too treatable and too ridiculous.

It's not every time you get diagnosed with cancer and it makes you laugh. I'd had a hemorrhoid operation. Two days later the colorectal surgeon called. "I'm sorry to tell you," he said, "your hemorrhoid was malignant."

"Malignant hemorrhoid?" I said. "There's no such thing as a malignant hemorrhoid."

"In almost every case you'd be right," the surgeon said and paused in a moment of sympathetic hesitation and of unintentional comic timing. "But . . ."

I laughed but I wanted to argue. "Malignant hemorrhoid" is Rush Limbaugh talk radio. "Malignant Hemorrhoid" is a Dave Barry rock band. But I still had to get treated. Going from the metaphysical to the all-too-physical reminded me of my gratitude to God. You have immediate access to the top specialist in the field when you pray. (Do polytheists have difficulties with this?) At least I had the good fortune to be in Washington, D.C.—a city full of flaccid old guys like myself who spend their time blowing smoke out of you-know-where and being full of you-know-what and sitting on their duffs. Consequently the town is full of medical expertise about the body part in question.

It turns out what I had was a skin cancer, squamous cell carcinoma. Practically every melanin-deficient (let alone Irish) person who spends time in the sun gets this if he or she lives long enough. "I call it 'adult acne' when it turns up on the face or arms," the oncologist said. But why it occasionally turns up where it turned up on me is something of a medical mystery. I mean, I was naked a lot in the 1960s but not *that* naked.

There's a considerable loss of dignity involved in trading the awe-inspiring fear of death for the perspiration-inducing fear of treatment. There are hells on earth. Until a generation ago the cure for anal cancer was a colostomy. Doctors have gotten over that. Most of the time. Now, with God's grace, the cure is radiation and chemotherapy. Would I have to go to some purgatorial place for this? To Sloan-Kettering in New York, a city I detest? Or out to the Mayo Clinic, although I have a phobia about hospitals named after sandwich toppings? "No," the oncologist said. "The treatment protocol is standardized and is successfully used everywhere."

I named my local New Hampshire hospital (and large animal veterinary clinic).

"Almost everywhere," the oncologist said.

I asked about the Dartmouth-Hitchcock Medical Center, ninety miles from my home but still on the planet New Hampshire. Dr. Marc Pipas at Dartmouth-Hitchcock's Norris Cotton Cancer Center came strongly recommended. Dr. Pipas is an avid bird hunter and an advocate of reintroducing the prairie chicken to the eastern seaboard. So he and I had something to talk about in addition to my behind. I'd need radiation therapy every day for six weeks. (Every day, that is, Monday through Friday—the radiology department has to play golf, too.) And I would undergo two four-day stints of around-the-clock chemotherapy, carrying a fanny pack of poisonous chemicals to be pumped into my body through a surgically implanted mediport. (Dr. Pipas persuaded the infusions department to install this on the left side of my chest so that it wouldn't interfere with mounting a shotgun.)

In theory I could get my radiation treatments elsewhere, within easy commuting distance. But it's worthwhile to find out what a doctor himself would do if he had your medical problem. And he probably thinks he does. Several doctor friends have told me you can't get through medical school without being convinced that you have every disease in the textbooks, including elephantiasis, beriberi, and guinea worm infestation. Dr. Pipas immediately said that, for anal cancer, he'd go to the radiologist Dr. Bassem Zaki at Norris Cotton Cancer Center.

Dr. Zaki is a Coptic Christian who immigrated from Egypt in his late teens. He and I talked about Middle Eastern politics, which, as far as I'm concerned, is the second most interesting blood sport after upland-game shooting.

Dartmouth-Hitchcock Medical Center is a sparkling edifice, full of light and air and surprisingly good art for a nonprofit institution. The architectural style is higgledy-piggledy 1980s modern—2 million square feet, every one of which is between you and where you have an appointment. Finding your way around is a trial run for Alzheimer's but a small price to pay for the pleasant surroundings. Even the food in the cafeteria is good. Various scientific studies have shown that patients recover better and faster in cheerful environments. Duh.

The staff at DHMC is also cheerful, but not *too* cheerful. The staff members don't make you feel like a small child at the receiving end of an overambitious preschool curriculum.

Perhaps they know better because DHMC is a teaching hospital. The Dartmouth Medical School is the fourth-oldest in the nation, founded in 1797. DHMC is venerable as well as modern. But not *too* venerable. It doesn't use leeches.

Being at a teaching hospital puts a patient in a comfortable equation with the institution. People are expecting to learn something from you, not just do something to you. But let's not push the idea of equality too far. There's a current notion that you should "take charge of your disease." No thanks. I'm busy. I've got cancer. I'm willing to face having cancer. I'm not willing to face having cancer with homework. I promised Dr. Pipas and Dr. Zaki that I wouldn't show up with sheaves of printouts from the Internet containing everything on Wikipedia about malignancies. They each laughed with detectable notes of relief. (Although I suspect my wife has made her way into the health blog ether. Fish oil pills, raw kelp, and other untoward substances started showing up on the dinner plates after I was diagnosed.)

Dr. Pipas and Dr. Zaki combined had something like half a century of medical experience. God wants us to have faith in what we can't see. Therefore He certainly wants us to have faith in what we can. I could see the diplomas on the doctors' office walls.

"I've got cancer" is more than an excuse for rational ignorance about medicine. It's an excuse for everything. From niece's wedding to daughter's piano recital to IRS audit, you're off the hook. I even tried my excuse on the Pope. I couldn't go to Mass because of the effect that germ-swapping Vatican II "sign of peace" handshakes could have on my radiation-weakened immune system. And I continued to employ cancer as an excuse until an exasperated spouse finally shouted, "You're curable! You *can too* put your dirty dishes in the sink!"

The radiation treatments weren't bad—twenty minutes propped on a machine in a humiliating posture. Most of me was exposed and the nurses were embarrassingly pretty. But it's interesting, the connection that physical modesty has with physical vanity. Once past sixty you can reasonably abandon both. This was one of the life lessons with which having cancer abounds. I hate life lessons. Consider all the I-hope-you've-learned-your-lesson experiences: skinned knees, high school romances, wreckage of dad's car, flunked college courses, horrible hangovers, failed marriages. I tell my children, "Avoid life lessons. The more important the lesson, the more you should avoid it."

The chemotherapy was worse than the radiation. The pump in the fanny pack of poisonous chemicals made a whining whirr every minute or so—not frequently enough to get used to and too frequently to let me sleep. A long plastic tube that attached the fanny pack to my mediport allowed me to bury the pump and its noise in a mound of pillows. But then I'd forget that I was connected. As with all attempts to forget one's troubles, I was courting disaster. I'd get up in the middle of the night to go to the bathroom and be yanked back to the mattress by the tubing. The fanny pack came with a bag of protective clothing and instructions for dealing with chemical spills. According to these instructions I was supposed to do, by myself, what the entire U.S. government had done during the 2002 national anthrax panic.

The cumulative effects of the treatments were unpleasant. The loss of my previously full, thick head of ungrayed hair met with no sympathy from my age cohort of males. I developed fatigue, mouth sores, and a rash around my loins as if I'd been dressed in nothing but hip boots and an Eisenhower jacket and turned on a spit in a tanning salon.

Suffering makes us question God. My question was: What evolutionary purpose does the itch serve? Indeed, an itch may be an argument for intelligent design. Maybe we itch not for biological purposes but to give us a moral lesson about surrendering to our strongest passions. I had the strongest passion to scratch certain parts of my body. If, however, I had scratched these parts of my body near a school or playground, I would be sent to jail.

Dr. Pipas, Dr. Zaki, and the Dartmouth-Hitchcock staff were attentive to my complaints and gave me generous doses of things to turn complaints into complaisance. But I was nagged by a concern about the quality of my medical care. Was it too good? I'm well insured and passably affluent. I asked Jason Aldous, Dartmouth-Hitchcock's media relations manager, "What if I weren't?"

"We're a charitable institution," Aldous said. "No one will ever be refused care here. On the other hand, we have to keep the lights on. We do try to find any possible means of payment—government programs, private insurance, et cetera."

The hospital has a whole department devoted to that. "In about sixty percent of cases," Aldous said, "people who think they aren't eligible for any assistance actually are." Then there are the people who have income but no savings, or assets but no income. Discounts are provided and payment plans worked out. Failing all else, treatment is simply given free—$63 million worth in 2007.

I asked Aldous about who gets what treatment from which doctor. Do your means affect the hospital's ways?

"The doctors," he said, "don't know how—or if—you're paying."

What Jason Aldous told me seemed true from what I could see of the hospital's patients, a cross section of Yankees, flinty and otherwise. The Norris Cotton Cancer Center alone treats more than 5,000 people a year. And we were all amiable in the waiting rooms. Anytime someone new came in and sat down he or she was tacitly invited to spend about three minutes telling everyone what was wrong. Then the conversation was expected to return to general topics. The general topic of choice during the summer of 2008 was how the Democrats would destroy the private health care system that was saving our lives. When medicine was socialized we'd have to sit in waiting rooms forever, if we lived. (The exception to the three-minute rule was for a child patient. Then there was unlimited interest and upbeat chat.)

In my case at least, the amiability had something to do with painkilling drugs, of which I was on plenty. Opiates are a blessing—and a revelation. Now when I see people on skid row nodding in doorways I am forced to question myself. Have they, maybe, chosen a reasonable response to their condition in life? Being addicted to drugs is doubtless a bad plan for the future, but having cancer also lets you off the hook about taking long-term views.

I'm sure that various holy martyrs and pious ascetics will disagree, but I saw no point to adding suffering to my suffering. And I can't say I had a sign from God that I should, at least not if God was speaking through my old friend Greg Grip.

Greg was baching it in a cottage on Lake Mascoma, fifteen minutes from Dartmouth-Hitchcock. He's divorced and his college-age daughter was away at a summer job. "I'm not saying you can stay at the cottage while you get treated," Greg said. "I'm saying I will be deeply offended if you don't."

Dr. Zaki arranged my radiation treatments, late on Monday afternoons and early on Friday mornings. My wife and children were spared self-pitiful weekday grousings. And I missed them, so I was on good behavior over weekends.

Greg is a splendid Weber grill cook. Charcoal fires produce carcinogens, but the chemotherapy had that covered. Dr. Pipas said I could have one measured Scotch each evening. But he failed to specify the measure. I think the pint is a fine old measure, although the liter is more up-to-date.

I couldn't tolerate the sun, but Greg's cottage is on the southwest shore of Mascoma. The patio was in shade all afternoon. I read a lot, mostly histories of World War II concerning the Russian front. Everyone on the Russian front in World War II was having it worse than I was.

Tony Snow, the former Bush administration press secretary, wrote an essay about dying from colon cancer. Tony said that the sense of mortality promoted "the ability to sit back and appreciate the wonder of every created thing." Every created thing put on a wonderful show for me at Lake Mascoma. A family of mergansers with six ducklings was living under the dock. A pair of mallards had taken up residence in the shrubbery. Beavers swam up and down the lake; I don't know why—Mascoma has a concrete dam. There were bird sightings—hawks, turkey vultures, kingfishers, a bald eagle, even an extremely wayward pelican. A hummingbird visited the patio every evening. Skinny-dipping sightings were also made at a nature reserve across the lake. Water skiers and Jet Ski riders took amusing falls. Not to engage in the pathetic fallacy, but the weather itself was kind and cool. Greg's pointer Weezy slept on my bed each night, though this may have had less to do with doggy compassion than the fact that Greg won't let her sleep on his. Weezy's dulcet snoring drowned out the chemo fanny pack pump.

I'm doing fine now. Anal cancer can be invasive, but mine seems to have had a wimpy EU-style foreign policy. The cancer is gone, as far as can be told. I still have a colonoscopy to worry about and a CAT scan to dread and six-month checkups to fret over. I'll be OK. Or I won't. Or I'll go through it all again.

This summer was not the worst summer of my life— loving family, kind friends, skilled and considerate care, a big warm dog in the bed. The worst summer of my life was forty years ago when I was young and healthy and didn't have a care in the world. But there was this girl, and a novel that refused to write itself, and anomie, and angst, and weltschmerz. . . . Nothing brings us closer to God than age and illness. I only hope the Almighty doesn't mind having nothing but sick old people around.

17

The Seventy-Two-Hour Afghan Expert
Kabul, July 2010

❖

If you spend seventy-two hours in a place you've never been, talking to people whose language you don't speak about social, political, and economic complexities you don't understand, and you come back as the world's biggest know-it-all, you're a reporter. What do you want to know about Afghanistan, past, present, or future? Ask me anything.

As all good reporters do, I prepared for my assignment with extensive research. I went to an Afghan restaurant in Prague. Getting a foretaste—as it were—of my subject, I asked the restaurant's owner (an actual Afghan), "So what's up with Afghanistan?"

He said, "Americans must understand that Afghanistan is a country of honor. The honor of an Afghan is in his gun, his land, and his women. You take a man's honor if you take his gun, his land, or his women."

And the same goes for where I live in New Hampshire. I inquired whether exceptions could be made, on the third point of honor, for ex-wives.

"Oh yes," he said.

Afghanistan—so foreign and yet so familiar and, like home, with such wonderful lamb chops. I asked the restaurateur about other similarities between New Hampshire and Afghanistan.

"I don't know," he said. "Most of my family lives in LA."

In Kabul I was met at the airport by M. Amin Mudaqiq, bureau chief for Radio Free Europe/Radio Liberty's Afghan branch, Radio Azadi. "Our office is just down the main road," he said, "but since it's early in the morning we'll take the back way, because of the Suicides." That last word, I noticed, was pronounced as a proper noun, the way we would say "Beatles" slightly differently than "beetles." And, in a sense, suicide bombers do aspire to be the rock stars of the Afghan insurgency (average career span being about the same in both professions).

"The Suicides usually attack early in the morning," Amin said. "It's a hot country and the explosive vests are thick and heavy."

I'd never thought about suicide bombing in terms of comfort. Here's some guy who's decided to blow himself gloriously to bits and he's pounding the pavement all dressed up in the blazing sun, sweat running down his face, thinking, "Gosh, this thing itches, I'm pooped, let's call it off."

"It's the same with car bombs," Amin said. "You don't want to be driving around the whole day with police everywhere and maybe get a ticket."

Imagine the indignity of winding up in traffic court instead of the terrorist equivalent of the Rock and Roll Hall of Fame.

Kabul is a walled city, which sounds romantic except the walls are precast reinforced concrete blast barriers, ten feet tall and fifteen feet long and moved into place with cranes. The walls are topped with sandbags and the sandbags are topped with guard posts from which gun barrels protrude.

Amin pointed out the sights. "There's UN headquarters." All I could see was blast barriers, sandbags, and gun barrels. "There's the German embassy"—barriers, bags, and barrels. "There's the embassy of China"—barriers, bags, and barrels. I spotted a rough-hewn stone fort on a hilltop, looking more the ancient way Kabul should look. "Oh, nineteenth-century British," Amin said.

Security, in various senses of the term, was all over the place. I have never seen so many types and kinds of soldiers, policemen, and private security guards or such a welter of uniforms, each in a different pattern of camouflage every one of which stuck out like a toreador's suit of lights against the white blast walls. Some of this security was on alert, some was asleep, some was spit-and-polish, some had its shoes untied, and some, rather unaccountably, was walking around without weapons.

None of the security was American. Americans don't patrol Kabul. The American military is suffering its usual fate, the same as it does at an army base in Georgia—shunted off to places the locals don't care to go.

The Kabul cityscape looks like a cornfield maze version of the old Berlin Wall without the graffiti, or like an unshelled Verdun gone condo with high-rise trenches. Afghanistan's capital is located in a grand hollow, as if someone had closed the Rockies in tight around Denver. On the slopes of Kabul's mountains there is another cityscape of small stone houses. They could be from the time of the Prophet, although they all seem to have aluminum window frames. This is where the poor live, with panes of glass to keep out the winter winds but not much else. At night you can see how far the electric wires run uphill—not very far. The water pipes don't go up at all, and residents—women and children residents, I'm sure—must climb from the bottom with their water.

Then, around the corner from the blast walls, there's a third Kabul, an ordinary city with stores and restaurants open to the street and parking impossible to find. The architecture is overseas modern in cement and chrome with some leftover Soviet modern in just cement. It looks a bit worn and torn but less so than Detroit or trans-Anacostia Washington, D.C. People are going about their business in Kabul with no apparent air of knowing that "people are going about their business in Kabul" is considered a very special thing at the U.S. State Department.

Security here is merely ubiquitous as opposed to omnipresent. Men, women, and children mingle. Women cover themselves in public but not more than my Irish great-aunts did at Mass. An occasional down-to-the-ground burka is seen but not as often as in London. In the malls, clothing shops predominate. Men's and women's clothes are shinier and more vividly colored than those seen in a traditional society such as New Hampshire.

Traditionalism being one of the things that makes Afghanistan so hard for Americans to understand. We Americans have so many traditions. For instance, our political traditions date back to the twelfth-century English Parliament if not to the Roman Senate. Afghans, on the other hand, have had the representative-democracy kind of politics for only six years. Afghanistan's political traditions are just beginning to develop. A Pashtun tribal leader told me that a "problem among Afghan politicians is that they do not tell the truth." It's a political system so new that this needed to be said out loud.

In the matter of opinion polling, however, Afghanistan is fully up-to-date. Concerning the popularity of President Hamid Karzai, the tribal leader said, "He is welcomed by bullets in many provinces." Of course, in America, this would be a metaphorical statement—except in 1865, 1881, 1901, 1963, 1981, etc.

The Pashtun tribal leader was one of a number of people whom Amin Mudaqiq arranged for me to interview. Tribalism is another thing that makes Afghanistan hard to understand. We Americans are probably too tribal to grasp the subtlety of Afghan tribal concepts. The Pashtun tribal leader was joined by a Turkmen tribal leader who has a PhD in sociology. I asked the Turkmen tribal leader about the socioeconomic, class, and status aspects of Afghan tribalism.

"No tribe is resented for wealth," he said. So, right off the bat, Afghans show greater tribal sophistication than Americans. There is no Wall Street Tribe upon which the Afghan government can blame everything.

I asked the Turkmen, "Did either the Communists or the Taliban try to use one tribe against another?"

"No," he said, "I didn't notice such a policy with the Soviets. And the Taliban does not publicly use tribalism."

Even the worst of Afghan governments never acquired the special knack of pitting tribe against tribe that is vital to American politics—the Squishy Liberal Tribe versus the Kick-Butt Tribe; the Indignantly Entitled Tribe versus the Fed-Up Taxpayer Tribe; the Smug Tribe versus the Wipe-That-Smirk-Off-Your-Face Tribe.

"We are all one nation," said the Pashtun tribal leader. "In the name of Afghan is included all the tribes of Afghanistan. Outsiders create divisions to serve their own interests." Better than having insiders create divisions to serve their own interests. President Obama, take note.

"Are there land issues between the tribes?" I asked the Turkmen. He told me there are land issues between *everybody*. Land titles are a mess in Afghanistan, or, as the Turkmen put it with a nice PhD turn of phrase, "Definition of ownership is originally ambiguous." The situation is so confused that the Soviets, of all people, attempted to impose private property in Afghanistan. "They tried to change the law, but the period was too short. Afghanistan," the Turkmen said, and laughed, "did not use the benefits of colonialism."

The problem in Afghanistan is really not so much land as water. It's a dry country with ample amounts of water running through it but not to good enough effect. "We have a law to distribute water but not to *manage* water," the Turkmen said. This lack of management combines with the age-old managerial conflicts between nomads who need watered pastures and farmers who need irrigation. Partly this is a nontribal matter, since there are both nomads and farmers in various tribes. But partly it is a tribal matter because of the different ways that tribes decide to cease to be nomads and become farmers.

"The Turkmen," said the Turkmen, "settle close to the desert. The Pashtuns settle close to the source of the water." Downstream and upstream. It's the plot of *Chinatown*. If you don't understand Afghanistan, blame Robert Towne.

Both the Pashtun tribal leader and the Turkmen tribal leader were unenthusiastic about the use of the word "tribal" and felt that "ethnic groups" is a better way to describe the differences among Afghans.

I held forth on American patriotism, how it had to do with our own ethnic groups, and the attempt to give American immigrants of the late nineteenth and early twentieth centuries a sense of nationhood. The tribal leaders understood exactly what I meant, which is more than I can say for our NATO allies on the subject of American patriotism.

"Fifty years ago," the Turkmen said, "things in Afghanistan were going in the same direction as the U.S. growth of patriotism. These systems were disturbed by the events of the last thirty years. Also, the geographical location of Afghanistan is not helpful to building national ideals. The focal points of the tribes are outside the country."

But not far enough outside. The Turkmen have their heartland in Turkmenistan, the Uzbeks in Uzbekistan, the Tajiks in Tajikistan and Iran. Even the Pashtuns, who are the largest ethnic group in Afghanistan, making up about 40 percent of the population, count Peshawar in the Northwest Territories of Pakistan as their cultural capital. And the language spoken by most educated Afghans, Dari, is a dialect of Persian. It is as if, around the time Emma Lazarus was penning "Give me your tired, your poor, your huddled masses yearning to breathe free," Dublin and Naples and Warsaw and Minsk had been moved—complete with every palace, slum, monument, gutter, princeling, priest, bum, thug, and man-at-arms—to Ellis Island, and all of America's schools had started teaching their lessons in French.

Nonetheless Afghan patriotism obtains. Maybe because, as the Turkmen tribal leader pointed out, every "old country" to which an Afghan ethnic might turn manages—somewhat extraordinarily—to be a worse place than Afghanistan.

There's that and what the Pashtun tribal leader had to say: "If Afghanistan is divided, why do we keep defeating outsiders?" He went on in that vein, like Lincoln but with 1,000 more years of history to go on, dating back to the twelfth-century outsider-defeating Afghan empire of Alauddin Husain, known as the "World-Burner." In the Pashtun's words, "A divided country cannot win."

Earlier in the day I'd heard a mullah become heated on the subject of ethnocentric politics. He accused a politician in the Karzai government of being a "national traitor" for doing what in the United States would be called playing the Charlie Rangel card. The politician is a member of the Hazara tribe (the Afghan politician, that is, though I'm sure Charlie Rangel would be glad to claim Hazara blood if it got him a tribal casino in New York's Fifteenth Congressional District). "Why I called him a national traitor," said the mullah, "is because he said he would shed his blood in favor of Hazaras. Instead of saying this was a judicial matter, he said it was a fighting matter. He broke his constitutional obligation."

The mullah represents another thing that makes Afghanistan hard to understand for Americans, although only for elite Americans who've had prestigious schooling and hold advanced opinions about everything. We ordinary Americans, far from such centers of heathen unbelief as the Brookings Institution, get the drift of a deeply religious polity.

I interviewed two mullahs at once. This might have been awkward, as they were opposite types, but they seemed fond of each other and the quieter mullah even took a few notes while the more voluble mullah was talking.

The quiet mullah was quietly dressed and modestly bearded, his close-cut hair topped with a simple turban. He was immediately recognizable as "mainstream." I don't mean he was hopelessly mainstream to the post-religious point, like some American clergy. I'd compare him to a solid Methodist or Presbyterian or picket-fence Baptist, not unwilling to make his sermons socially relevant but no electric guitars in the choir loft. "Preaching isn't limited to the mosque," he said, and told me how he spends time sitting with shopkeepers, listening to complaints about price gouging, and talking about the Islamic view of these matters. It is, by the way, things like price gouging that the Taliban casts itself as a defender against—the free market being one more of modernity's villains.

"I make the subjects of my sermons both Islamic and scientific," said the quiet mullah. "People are the enemy of those things they do not know." He talked about peace, not harping on its somewhat obvious convenience for individuals, but speaking of "the importance of peace to *Islam*." There's something more than mortal men at stake in peace—God demands it.

Along with peace, the mullah said, one of the most frequent topics of his sermons is leadership. He tries to explain, as a prayer leader, how to select a political leader. This is an easy enough colloquy to have with fellow Muslims. There is no generally accepted earthly hierarchy in Islam, especially in Sunni Islam, and there's certainly no pope. A Muslim may pray on any piece of ground. A mosque is an institution that adheres to the definition of a church given by Jesus: "Where two or three are gathered together." Muslims choose their own mosque, and, ideally at least, those who pray at that mosque choose their own mullah. People who say the Muslim world isn't ready for democracy ignore, among other things, the fact that Muslims already have it.

Two of the criteria that the quiet mullah gave for political leadership would eliminate most U.S. politicians: "Be educated. Know the society." But the first criterion was to be Muslim.

The more voluble mullah explained, "Since the time of Adam until now there are four books from God." (Muslims, like Jews, separate the Pentateuch from the rest of the Old Testament.) "This is our constitution."

It's a little long, I suppose—even longer than the proposed EU Constitution. But there are worse documents by which to live and govern—the proposed EU Constitution, for example.

Being a person who believes in God-given rights, I don't find a God-given constitution very disturbing. But some Americans—Americans involved in Afghan policy—apparently do. The next night I had dinner with the governor of a province that has its share of Taliban troubles. Talking about the hindrances he faces in getting assistance from the United States, the governor protested against something that he must have been told by some American, that there is a "ban on religion" in the U.S. Constitution.

"Disarm the Taliban," the governor said. "Take the Islamic weapon away from them." He wasn't talking about secularization.

"The best reason for belief," said the voluble mullah, "is that every country has its own laws. The death of a person is the beginning of another, greater journey—more dangerous than the journey you're taking now. Like police at the airport when you leave here, Allah will be asking the same way, 'Have you obeyed the law?'"

This mullah was a splendid figure, a big man in a bright white *shalwar kameez* with a magnificence of beard in elaborate curls and a turban that looked as if it would take all night to unwind and all day to wind up again. He was an evangelical. I say that in the original complimentary Gospel way. (I'm Low Church Protestant on my mother's side.) I was swept up with his eloquence before its translation arrived, when I didn't even know what he was saying. What he was saying was, "There is God. There is no rival to God, or there would have been an election or a coup d'état."

He was concerned that I'd made it only three-quarters of the way through the four books from God since the time of Adam. I was concerned that if I spent another twenty minutes with him I'd be in trouble with my parish priest.

I asked both mullahs about the idea of a "clash of civilizations" between Islam and the West. The quiet mullah thought there might be some truth in the notion, arising from three things: inappropriate behavior of Muslims, materialism (in the metaphysical sense) of non-Muslims, and mutual ignorance.

"Maybe," I volunteered, "the real clash of civilizations is between people who believe in God and people who don't."

The voluble mullah said, "There are those who don't believe in God. Fortunately neither Muslims or Afghans or Americans are among them." I hope he's not being too optimistic about the last named. (Later I would get a more dismissive answer to the question about the clash of civilizations, from a member of the Afghan parliament. He said, "Chinese, Muslims, Jews, Europeans—they work together in international finance markets every day.")

As the mullahs were departing, an Afghan journalist gestured toward the more prepossessing of the two. "He's a drone problem," said the journalist. "They see the clothes and the turban from up in the air and they think, 'Taliban!' And he *is* like Taliban, but on the good side."

Yet someone in Afghanistan must think the Taliban on the other side are good for something, too. Otherwise there wouldn't be an "Afghan issue."

The Taliban offer bad law—chopping off hands, stoning desperate housewives, the usual things. Perhaps you have to live in a place that has had no law for a long time—since the Soviets invaded in 1979—before you welcome bad law as an improvement. An Afghan civil society activist, whose work has put him under threat from the Taliban, admitted, "People picked Taliban as the lesser of evils." He explained that lesser of evils with one word, "stability."

A woman member of the Afghan parliament said that it was simply a fact that the Taliban insurgency was strongest "where the government is not providing services." Rule of law being the first service a government must provide.

The member of parliament who laughed at the clash of civilizations laughed as well at what has passed for rule of law in Afghanistan. "Sure, Afghanistan is unruly," he said. "Afghans don't like rules. No one likes rules. And that is what we have been—*ruled*. We have been *ruled*, not *governed*."

"The insurgency is also strongest," the woman member of parliament said, "where private security is stirring up trouble."

United States and NATO forces are also seen to have a hand in the churning. A Shia candidate for parliament said, "The Afghan people hate your troops when they support a corrupt governor or a warlord."

A journalist for Radio Azadi said, "Afghans were happy *in principle* that Americans brought peace and democracy. But when rival tribes began to use the U.S. to crush each other, the attitude of the Afghan people changed."

Afghans think Americans have sided with the wrong people. It's not that Afghans think Americans have sided with the wrong people in a systematic, strategic, or calculated way. It's just that we came to a place that we didn't know much about, where there are a lot of sides to be on, and we started siding with this side and that side and the other side. We were bound to wind up on the wrong side sometimes. We're outsiders in Afghanistan, and this is Occam's razor for explaining the Taliban. Imagine if America were a country beset with all sorts of intractable difficulties. Or don't imagine it—America *is* a country beset with all sorts of intractable difficulties. Our government is out of control, wantonly interfering in every aspect of our private lives and heedlessly squandering our national treasure at a time when Americans are suffering grave economic woes. Meanwhile vicious tribal conflicts are being fought for control of America's culture and way of life. (I've been watching FoxNews.)

What if some friendly, well-meaning, but very foreign power, with incomprehensible lingo and outrageous clothes, were to arrive on our shores to set things right? What if it were Highland Scots? There they go marching around wearing skirts and purses and ugly plaids, playing their hideous bagpipe music, handing out haggis to our kiddies, and offending our sensibilities with a lack of BVDs under their kilts. Maybe they do cut taxes, lower the federal deficit, eliminate the Department of Health and Human Services and the EPA, give people jobs at their tartan factories, and launch a manhunt for Harry Reid and the UC-Berkeley faculty. We still wouldn't like them. In New Hampshire there'd be more than one neighbor of mine up in his tree stand taking potshots at the Scotties with his deer rifle, especially if Jock left a nickel tip at the local diner for the neighbor's waitress wife.

Maybe my neighbor doing the shooting at silly ribboned bonnets isn't my favorite neighbor. Maybe he's the neighborhood jerk. But you can suppose how I might feel about my fellow Granite State nutcases, and I can suppose how Afghans might feel about the Taliban. They're assholes, but they're our assholes.

The Pashtun tribal leader said, "I tell my own tribesmen to not support the Taliban, but they don't listen. They see the Taliban as fighting invaders."

It's not just an invasion by soldiers that the Taliban could be seen as fighting. It's an invasion by a whole outlandish other world, as alien to Afghans as a lot of cable TV is to me. Indeed, the provincial governor said that people in villages will ask him, "Why is a naked fellow on television?" I said I'd like to know myself.

The journalist with Radio Azadi said, "When people felt they were dishonored, they needed revenge. The Taliban gave them revenge."

To fully sympathize with the dishonor an Afghan might feel, foreign government, UN, and NGO aid agencies must be considered. A myriad of them operate in Afghanistan, staffed by people from around the globe. So it's not just that you've got Highland Scots marching in hairy-kneed formations up and down your subdevelopment's cul-de-sac. Many of the most ordinary functions of your society have been taken over by weird strangers. When you need a flu shot or a dog license or a permit to burn leaves, you have to go see Bulgarians and Bolivians and Nigerians and Fiji Islanders. Some Mumbai babu is sitting on your zoning board saying, "Oh my gosh golly no, it is most inefficient use of land to forbid parking of the camper vans on war memorials."

Afghanistan's minister of education, Farooq Wardak, is no friend of the Taliban, but he did sound like a potential recruit for the Tea Party. "I am absolutely unhappy with the U.S. role in Afghan education," he said. "Zero percent of U.S. aid to Afghan education is spent through the Afghan government."

"Why?" I asked.

"Because the Ministry of Education is not certified by USAID because no one from USAID has evaluated me or my ministry in the two years that I've held the job." Without the evaluation he can't get the certification.

He said that the U.S. government wanted to spend money on a program called "Community-Based Education." But that was a program the ministry had developed when the Taliban were attacking girls' schools across Afghanistan.

It was a way to provide, he said, "covert education for girls. Now we need overt schools."

The U.S. also wants to spend money, he complained, on "accelerated teacher training" when what Afghanistan needs is just plain teacher training. "Either give the money to us or align with the program," he said. "This accelerated training leaves no bricks and mortar behind. You are spending U.S. tax dollars building something taxpayers can't see." His pocket critique of U.S. aid: "Everything is air, nothing is on the ground." I didn't have the heart to tell him about No Child Left Behind back in America.

But the Taliban aren't winning much love, either—otherwise we and our NATO allies would have already gone the way of the Soviets. The civil society activist had a very Afghan insult for the Taliban: "The Taliban has the power to kill, and people still don't like them."

Radio Liberty's Pakistan bureau, which broadcasts in Pashto, had just run a story about the Taliban being as clumsy as the United States in dealing with tribalism—as clumsy but much more brutal. Unable to penetrate Pashtun tribal hierarchies, the Taliban had, according to the report, begun killing tribal elders, with more than 1,000 murdered so far.

"The older tribal leaders are everyone's target," the woman member of parliament said. She also described how the Taliban, in areas under their control, go to villagers and demand, "Son or money." This insistence on either payoff or cannon fodder (drone fodder, I suppose) must undercut the Taliban's reputation for incorruptibility. But corruption in the Afghan government remains a raw material of insurgency.

As I mentioned, there's a lot of security in Kabul. The only place I saw that lacked any security—not a gun or a goon to be seen—was at the office of the Shia candidate for parliament, Ramazan Bashardost. He has a reputation for fanatical opposition to corruption. And, actually, he doesn't have an office; he refuses to have an office. Instead he has a tent pitched across the street from the parliament building, a large, simple nomad's tent staked in an empty lot and without so much as a carpet on the stony ground.

Bashardost has something of the look of a young Ralph Nader, with that Nader gleam of indignation in his eyes and that Nader tendency to pull out thick sheaves of documentation concerning each subject he's indignant about. He had been in the parliament before. He quit over what might seem a fine point. "I left Parliament because Karzai said salaries should run through September when Parliament had ended in May."

He had also been minister of planning. "I left the Ministry of Planning for my values," he said. He pointed to the pavement between his tent and the fortified parliament building. The four-lane avenue was completely torn up, littered in construction machinery, and nearly impassable. "We are three years into a six-month road project."

Asked to summarize corruption in Afghanistan, he said, "It is a Mafia economy disguised as a market economy."

Not that Bashardost is at all like Ralph Nader is his attitude toward a market economy. He has a PhD in economics and believes Afghanistan should be using private investment for development rather than international aid. But, he said, "Afghans hate a 'market economy' because it equals corruption." (Being fluent in English, he put "market economy" into phonetic quotation marks. He did the same with "democracy.") "Afghans hate 'democracy' because democracy equals power of the warlords, equals power of corruption, equals no rule of law."

If Americans claim not to understand Afghan corruption, we're lying. Bribery has been a dominant part of our foreign policy in Afghanistan, the way it's been a dominant part of everyone's foreign policy in Afghanistan, including al Qaeda's. What we Americans don't understand about Afghan corruption is why it's so transparent, just a matter of taking money. Don't the Afghans know that you should take bribes indirectly—by collecting publicity, popularity, public recognition, prestige, influence, and, most of all, power? Then big corporations put you on their boards of directors and *that's* when you get the money. Meanwhile you've been riding in government cars, flying on government planes, eating out of the government pork barrel (lamb barrel in Afghanistan), so why worry about payoffs up front?

Afghans have failed to move their corruption from the Rod Blagojevich model, which we all deplore, to the Barack Obama model, which we all admire. Afghanistan should, as the minister of education says, "align with the program."

How can we know what America should do in Afghanistan? I've returned fully informed on this subject as well. We should stay. The member of parliament who dismissed the clash of civilizations said, "It's like buying a beautiful home somewhere and letting your neighborhood deteriorate."

Really, seriously, we should stay. Otherwise, Ramazan Bashardost said, "You'll see Chinese soldiers in the street. We have a border with China. They're a very rich country. We're very poor people—in a most strategic region."

We should leave. The Pashtun tribal leader said, "We don't have war. What we have is instability. Armies create instability. If you try this for twenty more years you'll never succeed."

We should do both. One of the journalists with Radio Azadi said, "There's the same feeling in Afghanistan as there is in the U.S. We worry about the U.S. staying, and we worry about the U.S. leaving."

The Afghan people are pro-American. The woman member of parliament said, "We say, 'Our enemy is their enemy.'"

The Afghan people are anti-American. Ramazan Bashardost said, "Frankly, people are generally against the U.S." But he tries to argue with them. "I say U.S. troops are in Afghanistan for values, not for oil—there is not enough of it."

Afghans know that we are still committed to our mission in Afghanistan. The minister of education said, "I have complete faith. But whether we are able and smart enough to express this mission to the people of Afghanistan . . ." He let his words trail off.

Afghans don't know that we're still committed to our mission in Afghanistan. The provincial governor said, "If perception is created by your actions that democracy is against Islam, that a controlled insurgency is all that's wanted, that Afghanistan is being used as a jump point for other geopolitical concerns—that justifies the insurgency."

Afghans hope like heck that we're still committed to our mission in Afghanistan. The woman member of parliament said, "From 2001 to 2004 people were very optimistic. With the switch to Iraq things began to change."

Afghans can't live on hope alone. The voluble mullah said, "There is a saying, 'A blind man will not lose his stick twice.' But the people of Afghanistan have lost their stick twenty times."

We should talk to the Taliban. The Pashtun tribal leader said, "Accept the fact that we cannot eliminate all Taliban from Afghanistan."

We shouldn't talk to the Taliban. The governor said, "Talks further strengthen the enemy's position."

We must fight the war the Afghan way. The governor said, "The Taliban are very quick. Our current units need too much preparation to move."

We must fight the war the American way. The governor also said, "There is an Arab proverb about fear as a tactic: 'I win the war a month away.'" And the U.S. military has been doing some fearsome things for month upon month in Afghanistan.

The Afghan government can be reformed from within. The governor said, "Blaming corruption is just a way to put blame on others for our own shortcomings. Internal strategies are needed to strengthen military and civil society."

The Afghan government can't be reformed from within. Bashardost proposed something like what General MacArthur did in Japan after World War II.

Poverty is the root of Afghanistan's problems. Bashardost said, "We are ready to support you for three hundred years. *If* we have electricity. *If* we have a life."

Poverty is not the root of Afghanistan's problems. "Or Haiti would be the most terroristic country in the world," the governor said.

There must be *something* in Afghanistan that we've got right. There is. Radio Azadi, the Afghan bureau of Radio Free Europe/ Radio Liberty, is on the air twelve hours a day, seven days a week, half the time in Pashto, half the time in Dari. What Radio

Azadi does is known as "surrogate broadcasting," meaning the content is Afghan-produced as a way for Afghans to get news and views in a place where, otherwise, these have to be delivered mostly face-to-face. And there is no agenda except to be factual (although facts are an agenda item if you care about freedom, which is what Azadi means in Dari).

Radio Azadi's bureau chief, and my host in Kabul, Amin Madaqiq, has 120 staff members and freelancers. They produce news bulletins, news in depth, and features on social, political, and economic topics, plus a couple of hours a day of Afghan music and even some comedy: "Police announced today that all the people who have passed their driver's license test must now learn to drive."

A missing persons program, *In Search of a Loved One,* tries to reunite families separated by decades of chaos. A medical program is hosted by doctors with eminent specialists, often from overseas, as guests. *Azadi and Listeners* is devoted to getting individuals individual responses from government ministries.

The call-in shows are popular. On a day when I was in the studio Afghanistan's minister of communications and minister of the interior were taking random phoners, trying to clear up confusion about a confusing-sounding system of national ID cards. I don't think it's likely that the head of the FCC and a member of President Obama's cabinet would spend two hours in a spartan, airless broadcast booth helping people who are unable to read through a form-filling process and suggesting work-arounds when local government corruption is encountered.

The quiet mullah told me that the day before an elderly religious scholar had asked for help buying a radio so that Azadi could be listened to in his mosque.

The Pashtun tribal leader said, "Azadi is doing very well because they are telling the facts." He griped that other media were insensitive to religion and culture.

The civil society activist thought that wisdom and social relationships were best established in person, but second best was radio. "Radio can pass wisdom," he said.

The woman member of parliament told me about how, after the fall of the Taliban, Radio Azadi had conducted four hours a week of open political debate. "The Afghans *got it*," she said. She praised Azadi's "diversity of opinion" and the fact that it sometimes has "the government getting upset."

"Even the U.S. ambassador is afraid of our show," an Azadi journalist told me with a big smile.

"Any feeling of censorship from the U.S.?" I asked Amin.

"We haven't felt any," he said.

"A good channel," the minister of education called it. "An important institution. I've never had the feeling it was unnecessarily taking sides in the Afghan conflict. It maintains its impartiality."

"I wasn't sure what you'd hear from the minister," a journalist with Radio Azadi told me later. "We've been critical of him."

The member of parliament to whom I'd talked about clashing civilizations and deteriorating neighborhoods was a bit surprised at America sponsoring Azadi, the more so, I think, because he's an American. That is, he lived for a long time in America, where he spent ten years as a commercial airline pilot.

"America," he said, not without pride, "is spending money for you to express your opinions—not to twist your opinions but to *express* your opinions."

Ramazan Bashardost's only complaint about Radio Azadi

was that he wasn't on it often enough. He was reminded that, only recently, he had been named by Radio Azadi as "Person of the Year."

"Yes," he said, and apologized for bringing too much documentation to radio interviews. "One positive point in Afghanistan is media," he said. "And the only positive point in Afghanistan is media."

Even the Taliban call in to Radio Azadi—to argue with the hosts and guests.

"We know you are funded by the U.S. Congress," a Taliban spokesman told Amin. "But we judge you by your deeds."

"The Taliban call to argue—this is *good*," said the woman member of parliament.

"The Taliban fights the U.S. militarily," said the former airline pilot, "but uses the U.S. media to express themselves." He chuckled. "I say to them, 'If this system is bad, you are using it! When you had your radio, would you let *us* call in?'" He saw the Taliban as caught in a trap by the logic of freedom. "This is a format that must be expanded."

The governor thought the Taliban itself might accidentally expand it. He recalled the days before Radio Azadi, during Taliban rule, when the only outside media was the BBC Afghan service. "The Taliban told people that they would go to hell if they listened to the BBC. Then *everyone* listened."

There was one other point that people in Kabul agreed on. Whatever it is that America does in Afghanistan, America should proceed with wisdom. The governor told a story about wisdom.

There was a student who had been studying for many years at a madrassa. He had memorized the Qu'ran and learned all the lessons his teacher taught. One day he went to his teacher and said, "I am ready to leave and go be a mullah."

His teacher said, "I think you should stay here for a few more years."

"Why?" asked the student. "Is there some additional degree or higher certificate that I will get?"

"No," said the teacher, "all you will get is wisdom."

"But I'm ready to be a mullah now," said the student. And he left the madrassa and wandered from village to village looking for a mosque where he could be the prayer leader.

Finally the student came to a village where a corrupt old mullah was using the mosque as a stall for his cow. The student was outraged. He gathered the villagers together and told them, "I have studied at a madrassa. I have memorized the Qu'ran. It is a great sacrilege for your mullah to use the mosque as a stall for his cow." The villagers beat him up.

The student limped back to the madrassa and told his teacher what had happened. The teacher said, "Follow me." They went back to the village where the mullah was using the mosque as a stall.

The teacher gathered the villagers together and told them, "I see you have a beautiful cow being kept in your mosque. It must be a very blessed animal. And I hear the cow belongs to your mullah. He must be a very holy man. In fact, I think that this cow is so blessed and your mullah is so holy that if you were to take one hair from the cow's hide and one hair from the mullah's beard and rub them together, you would be assured of paradise."

The villagers ran into the mosque and began plucking hairs from the cow's hide. The cow started to buck and kick and it bolted from the mosque and disappeared. Then the villagers ran to the corrupt old mullah's house and began plucking hairs from his beard. And they tugged and they yanked so hard at the mullah's beard that he had a heart attack and died.

"You see," said the teacher to the student. "No cow in the mosque and a need for a new mullah—*that* is wisdom."

18

Capital Gains

Washington, D.C., August 2010

❖

We take the kids to Washington once or twice a year. In fact, Muffin and Poppet were born there, and until 2005 we split our time between an apartment in Washington and Breakwind Oaks, our house in New Hampshire's Beige Mountains. Eventually teachers lost their sense of humor about children being pulled out of school when New Hampshire got too cold and icy (October) and reinserted when Washington got too hot and muggy (March). We gave up the apartment and resigned ourselves to being year-round summer people in a state with no summer.

The kids still have friends in Washington and so do Mrs. O. and I, even if they do look at us funny when we arrive at the Capital Grill in muck boots and six layers of fleece and talk about what the hens, instead of the congressmen, are laying. Yet, although our children had been to Washington, they'd never BEEN TO WASHINGTON. That is, they'd never gone on the formal pilgrimage to our nation's capital, the expedition through history and civics that is all but mandatory for our country's young people and which, when not provided by parents, is supplied by the junior high class trip. Our kids hadn't yet journeyed to Washington for the specific purpose of being awed by America's saga-filled past, august institutions of democratic government, and many public buildings with lots of columns in the front.

Mrs. O. and I had each gone with our families, I in the 1950s, she in the 1970s. My memories of the experience remain vivid to this day. We toured the FBI building and got to see a machine gun fired. And we stayed in a hotel. "We stayed in a hotel!" I endlessly told my friends back in Toledo, when I wasn't endlessly telling them I'd seen a machine gun fired. I confess that many of the rest of my memories are not so vivid. I was impressed by how thick the piece of glass was over the top of the Declaration of Independence. The Smithsonian had the better part of a railroad train indoors. The lantern that hung from the front porch of the White House was huge. At the hotel you could call on the telephone and a man brought ice cream.

Mrs. O. did not think so much of the FBI building. Her father was an FBI agent, so they got the special tour that went on forever. To Mrs. O. it was as if Dagwood had taken Cookie to Mr. Dithers's office. She liked the room in the Smithsonian devoted to the first ladies' ball gowns. She can still recall a multitude of details about color, fabric, and style, if you let her.

"Our kids need these vivid memories," I said to Mrs. O. I decided that this time when we went to Washington we would be real tourists.

I immediately encountered resistance from the children. When I suggested a sightseeing excursion on one of the fake trolleys that lumber around the Mall, Muffin, age twelve, rolled her eyes so far back in her head that I wanted to ask her what the medulla oblongata looks like. "We used to live here, Dad," she sighed.

"What kind of sightseeing is seeing sights you've always seen?" asked Poppet, age ten.

"It's ninety-two degrees," said Mrs. O.

Buster, six, is usually game for anything on wheels, but he eyed the trolley and said, "That's a dumb bus."

We'd been through the White House the previous Christmas to see the holiday decorations, which were, to put it politely, Texan. The kids weren't impressed. There's some nut in the nearby town of Quaintford, New Hampshire, who has Mr. and Mrs. Claus and all the little Clauses on his roof along with a real sleigh drawn by the full complement of reindeer, Dancer through Rudolph, plus the Grinch and *his* sleigh over the garage and twenty giant candy canes made from old phone poles in his yard, all of this covered in blinking red and green lights, giving him an electric bill in an amount that would alarm Ben Bernanke and a long-running fight with the local zoning board. The Christmas White House was drab by comparison.

Mrs. O. and I remember thinking how big the White House was. Not our children. They're used to the neighboring summer places in the Beige Mountains, built when that region was a fashionable retreat for the more cracked type of Boston Brahmin. These dwellings cover acres with their cobwebs, dry rot, curling shingles, falling roof slates, and various wings that have been boarded up since the Gilded Age. We emerged from the White House at dusk. "Where are the bats?" said Poppet.

The kids had had a tour of the Capitol building, too, given by our then-senator John Sununu. He is a vigorous guide who loves the place and knows everything about it, but what the kids liked best was getting their photograph taken with the senator—because he signed his name "Sununununununu."

We couldn't get into the FBI building, no matter the wire-pulling by Mrs. O.'s father. Something about construction activity or the security situation or security activity in the construction situation. I doubt the FBI's liability lawyers let them fire machine guns anymore anyway.

The ranks of tour buses idling in a reek of diesel smoke and disgorging cargoes of fat rubbernecks camcording each other in their gigantic sports jerseys, balloon shoes, and fashion mistake shorts spoiled the quiet majesty of the Lincoln Memorial. And the emphasis on Sally Hemings in our children's history lessons spoiled the quiet majesty of the Jefferson Memorial.

The Air and Space Museum was great, of course, but we always go there. Buster and I like things that go fast and explode. And Mrs. O. and the girls get a kick out of hearing Daddy make dive-bomber noises.

In the end, by way of being real tourists, we went to the National Museum of American History. Built in 1964, the museum is ugly in a way that's best described as built in 1964. The ill-proportioned exterior slab walls are covered in prolix quotations from historical Americans. It takes longer to read the building than it took the architectural firm of McKim, Mead, and White to design it.

Inside the front doors was an exhibit of random guitars and a folk musician playing folk music. Folk music had an enormous impact on American history, causing the North to win the Civil War documentary by Ken Burns. Also, Woody Guthrie had a guitar with "This Machine Kills Fascists" carved on it, although the guitar probably would have been broken if any fascists actually had been killed. But maybe the guitar did get broken, because it wasn't in the exhibit. At least I don't think so. Not that we looked very hard.

Mrs. O. and the girls headed straight for the first ladies' ball gowns. An attempt had been made to add relevance to this exhibit. "Includes material related to their social and political activities," read a placard at the entrance. I dragged Buster to the exit to see if Hillary Clinton's ball gown was on display. Wasn't there some kerfuffle about this in 1993? Didn't Hillary Clinton think the First Lady clothes horse thing was beneath the dignity of the office (not that first ladies technically hold office) or sexist or something? And she wasn't going for that. But there was Hillary Clinton's ball gown nonetheless. Trailer park burka.

Buster and I retreated to a bench outside, where we contemplated Horatio Greenough's monumental sculpture of George Washington. Washington is depicted in the classical manner, half naked with his toga slipping. I don't think of George Washington as somebody who went around with his shirt off much. "Did he just get out of the bathtub?" Buster asked.

Poppet darted out from among the ball gowns looking worried about the prospect of adult womanhood. "What if they want to get on a teeter-totter or go down a slide?"

Muffin, although she is more fashion-conscious, or because she is more fashion-conscious, escaped soon after. "Stupid," she said.

Mrs. O. was in there for an hour. She emerged confirmed in her philosophical conservatism. "There's no such thing as progress," she said. "If I were to take a stylish Martian woman through that exhibit backward, starting with Michelle Obama's off-the-shoulder bedsheet and winding up with Abigail Adams, the Martian woman would be convinced that I was showing her the story of a society's gradual development of sophistication and good taste."

The Hall of Invention conveyed the same reverse message, beginning with marvelous things like mechanical wheat reapers and finishing with "How a Stroller Is Designed." How strollers are designed so that parents invariably get their fingers pinched when folding the strollers was not explained. Women and minority inventors were emphasized. Another exhibit was "The House." All it contained was pictures of and objects from what seemed to be the house where I grew up in the 1950s and 1960s. (Although the people depicted as living in my house were improbably racially integrated and dads were doing more housework than ever happened.) What interest could anyone have in looking at my house in the 1950s and 1960s? The less so since everyone visiting the museum had grown up in a house just like it or had parents or grandparents who did. Many of those houses are still around, much the same as they always were. I suppose "The House" had something to do with being interested in ordinary middle-class life or making ordinary middle-class life interesting, this being of interest to extraordinary non-middle-class museum curators. But John Hughes's movies do a better job.

"The History of Transportation" was sponsored by General Motors, so it was the history of cars, trucks, buses, and locomotives made by General Motors. Your tax dollars paying to bail out a corporation that's paying for an exhibit at a museum so that the museum doesn't have to spend your tax dollars—a nice Third-Way social democracy touch.

Buster and I were blissfully surrounded by cars. A great thing about being sixty-two years old and having a six-year-old son is that there's still somebody you can impress. "When I was a kid we owned one of these," I said. "And one of these and one of these and one of these . . ." (My father was a car dealer.)

Poppet likes the round-fendered models from just after World War II. "They're cuddly."

Muffin prefers the styling exuberance of the late 1950s. She said, of a 1959 Cadillac Eldorado convertible, "Justin Bieber should drive one."

"With the top up," said her little sister, "because of his girlie hair."

Mrs. O. travels forty miles a day delivering kids to school and picking them up. She was interested in the old streetcars. "Or anything else that's on rails, so I could read a book or something."

It was a fine exhibit despite the Museum of American History doing what it could to spoil the mood by using every excuse to present text and videos about segregation in public transport. It's not something the transportation did. Trains, Greyhound buses, farm pickups, and old jalopies got millions of black Americans out of the segregated South.

We went to see the Star-Spangled Banner. Older readers will remember when this hung on a wall in the Smithsonian. (And that wonderful Charles Addams house/nation's attic is no more. The original Smithsonian building has been turned into, I quote our guidebook, "an information center with video orientations.") The Star-Spangled Banner hung on the wall, and if you were nine, as I was when I visited Washington, you stood there agape, saying, "Wow. It's the Star-Spangled Banner whose broad stripes and bright stars through the perilous fight, o'er the ramparts we watched were so gallantly streaming. And it's right here hanging on the wall. Wow."

Not any more. The Star Spangled Banner has undergone "eventification." It's not about what you're going to see, it's about the journey. We entered a labyrinth darkened to pre-dawn's early light degree and cluttered with ancillary displays—"Baltimore in the Balance"—every one of them interactive as all get-out. We were bumping around in there for fifteen minutes, almost forgetting why, when Muffin mumbled, "Oh, there's the flag." It reclined on a semi-elevated surface as if on a hospital bed and was illuminated sporadically by only a dim light to prevent UV damage, never mind the rockets' red glare that our national colors had survived handily. It's not nearly as big as the AIDS quilt displayed on the Mall a few years back.

"How the heck are they going to work women and minorities into the Star-Spangled Banner?" asked Mrs. O. The answer was around the corner in an interactive display devoted to the seamstress Mary Pickersgill: "Her daughter, two nieces, and an African-American indentured servant helped piece together its 'broad stripes and bright stars.'" A plaque by the exit proclaimed that the principal donor for the Star-Spangled Banner installation was Ralph Lauren. If his company were based in Canada, with its "time to rake the leaves" ensign, he'd be shit out of luck with his logo.

We poked around in the museum for a while, a very little while, longer.

"That was boring," said Muffin as we left.

"Really boring," said Poppet.

"Really, really boring," said Buster.

We could persuade the kids to visit no further tourist attraction. Muffin and Poppet (and Mrs. O.) were more interested in shopping opportunities—something rural New Hampshire offers in the variety of animal fodder available at the feed store. Even Buster preferred the mall to the Mall. And we all wanted to see our friends. Some of these friends have swimming pools, an unheard-of thing in the Beige Mountains, where it would require the output of the Vermont Yankee nuclear power plant to heat one to fifty degrees in August.

As I floated in the pool, a gin fizz balanced on my paunch, I reflected that a liking for free enterprise, civil society, and material comforts as opposed to a liking for august institutions of democratic government indicated that none of my family will stray far from the GOP verities of life.

On our way to the airport, as we turned onto Memorial Bridge, Muffin asked, "What's the point of the Washington Monument?" "Five hundred and fifty-five feet, five and one-eighth inches," said Mrs. O., consulting our guidebook.

19

HOME UNALONE

New Hampshire, March 2011

School break loomed and the children were agitating for a vacation trip. Mrs. O. and I are tired of traveling with kids. They get peevish, bored, and quarrelsome, and they never want to go to where we want to go to, such as out for a late dinner at the Brasserie Lipp in Paris followed by a stroll across the boulevard and a nightcap at Café Flore.

"A cruise ship with an indoor climbing wall!" demanded Muffin.

"Disney World, Sea World, and Hogwarts at Universal Studios!" insisted Poppet.

"We should go to Nickelodeon!" declared Buster, who gets confused about geography.

"We have Nickelodeon at *home*," said Poppet, giving Mrs. O. and me an idea. Home is a fashionable watering hole for the elite these days. High-powered executives brag about working from home. A stay-at-home mom is a status symbol. Home entertainment centers fill the cathedral-ceilinged great rooms of America. Why not home travel? Reservations aren't a problem; the mortgage company has us booked for thirty years. No need to pack light; we all bring everything we own home. And meals are absolutely guaranteed to be had in a comfortable, homey atmosphere.

We lined up the children in the front hall and had them march shoeless through the door frame four or five times while emptying their pockets. "Gummi Bears are allowable only in containers of three ounces or less and must be sealed in a ziplock bag," said Mrs. O., giving the kids a sharp frisk. Meanwhile I repeatedly droned, "Please report any suspicious objects to police or TSA representatives" and "Curbside is for active loading and unloading only, unattended cars will be ticketed and towed."

We squeezed the kids into the third-row seat of our SUV, piling their laps with iPods, DVD players, Game Boys, and coloring books. I drove up and down our long, bumpy driveway for hours with occasional halts outside the garage for "minor maintenance delays." Mrs. O. grudgingly passed out peanuts.

"Time zone change," announced Mrs. O. when we were back inside. "It's four p.m. Everybody go to bed."

In the morning we dialed the thermostat to "Florida." The Orlando Amusement Park experience was easily evoked. Line up the kids again and leave them standing there for ages. Eventually they expect something in the way of a ride. Fortunately ours is an old house. There's a large, loud, and scary nineteenth-century toilet in the guest room bath. Our children were greeted by big, furry, overfriendly animal characters. "Dad," said Poppet, "those are our dogs."

"Yes," I said, "and you can have your picture taken with them. As for evening fireworks, don't get your father started about Eric Holder."

Going on a cruise with children means seasickness and sunburn. We convinced the kids to spin themselves around 100 times, then stand too close to the fireplace.

Mrs. O. emptied all the leftovers from the fridge onto the dining room table, creating a twenty-four-hour free buffet with authentic tourism-style discolored slices of lunch meat, wilted lettuce, and melted frozen yogurt. No cooking for Mom for a week!

We don't have an indoor climbing wall, but the ascent to our second floor is steep. We put ropes and bike helmets on the kids and let them climb the stairs. "Take some laundry with you when you go."

"Real cruise ships have hot tubs," Muffin complained.

"Get in the water," I said. "It's hot, it's a tub. What's the problem?"

Our children turned out to be every bit as peevish, bored, and quarrelsome during home travel as they usually are when traveling. But we saved money. In fact, Mrs. O. and I saved enough money to hire a very reliable, if somewhat strict, professional nanny to stay with the kids. We'll be at the Brasserie Lipp.